The Political Economy of Economic Performance

The Political Economy of Economic Performance

Sub-Saharan Africa before the Global Recession and the Way Forward

Voxi Heinrich Amavilah

LEXINGTON BOOKS
Lanham • Boulder • New York • London

Published by Lexington Books
An imprint of The Rowman & Littlefield Publishing Group, Inc.
4501 Forbes Boulevard, Suite 200, Lanham, Maryland 20706
www.rowman.com

6 Tinworth Street, London SE11 5AL, United Kingdom

British Library Cataloguing in Publication Information Available

Library of Congress Cataloging-in-Publication Data Available

Includes bibliographic references and index
ISBN 978-1-4985-9783-8 (cloth)
ISBN 978-1-4985-9784-5 (electronic)

Contents

List of Figures and Tables

FIGURES

TABLES

Preface

When the world economy was in bad shape during the mid-1970s and the late 1980s, especially following the US-Iran crisis and the Arab-Israeli oil embargo, the economic situation was many times worse for sub-Saharan African countries (SSACs) than it was for the rest of the world (ROW). Through 1986, for instance, the average annual growth rate of SSACs was either declining or negative compared to three plus percent for the ROW. It went up for the next two years, and down for the next four. After 1992, however, the rate of growth of SSACs picked up, surpassing the average rate for the ROW by 2000. Many experts, including the World Bank and International Monetary Fund (IMF), began to talk of a permanent turnaround for the SSACs. The 2007–2010 financial and economic crises—together the Great Global Recession (GGR)—mostly in the developed countries spread quickly to the developing countries via known channels and slowed down economic performance everywhere. However, "in [*sic*] previous global downturns, Sub-Saharan Africa has usually been badly affected—but not this time" (Sayeh 2012, 1). In fact, even post-GGR, in 2015 Africa's growth rate was still unusually high, convincing some to write of "the twilight of the resource curse" (Economist 1/7/2015, 1). Edwards, Johnson and Weil (2016) has since written a four-volume account of "African successes" focusing on "government and institutions" (Volume 1), "human capital" (Volume 2), "modernization and development" (Volume 3), and "sustainable growth" (Volume 4). The successes appear to have deep roots, because, while there was a strong correlation between commodity prices and GDP growth in Africa during the 1961–2014 years, with commodity prices leading the way, except during the mid-1970-early-1990s, GDP grew faster than commodity prices in the

"Africa rising" period (Arias and Wen 2015). "The twilight of the resource curse" is the idea that African economies have diversified away from commodities and toward telecommunication, transportation, and finance such that even African billionaires have made their money in these new areas.

It remains clear to-date that the "Africa rising" experience put many African countries on their positive performance trajectories unseen in many years past. Many experts have credited improvements in macroeconomic policy and reform in these countries as reasons for growth, but few among them have given satisfactory explanations. This is the phenomenon which interests the essays in this book. The essays fill the gap in current understanding of the performance of SSACs. They outline some factors and forces behind the good performance of SSACs, and sketch the way forward. All-in-all the essays suggest two broad themes—a weakness that represents an unavoidable tradeoff between depth and breadth. The first theme is about the factors and forces responsible for performance. These include (a) the intensity of use of newer technologies (mainly mobile phones and the internet); (b) the gathering importance of technical knowledge; (c) the role of conventional factors and forces of production (both local and global); and (d) the quality of institutions.

The significance of the intensity of use of newer technologies suggests that the obstacle to the good economic performance of SSACs is not lack of technology, but rather the difficulty of spreading technology and its underlying knowledge from advanced to developing countries and even within SSACs themselves. Therefore, the second theme of the book focuses on the way forward. First, it characterizes the problems that frustrate the spread of knowledge and technological innovations. Last, it stresses resource intra-actions and interactions as sources of technological change and long-run economic growth.

Each essay stands alone, making some repetition unavoidable. However, since a main objective of the book is to provoke a positive (encouraging) positive (objective) inquiry into the performance of SSACs, I hope some repetition provides a reasonably general perspective within which other studies can proceed. Thus, although the scope is SSACs, I believe the book is suitable for all readers interested in the economic performance of developing countries for research and policy reasons. However, it is most suitable for advanced undergraduate and graduate students in economic development and related fields, academic libraries with an Africa focus, and for policymakers both in SSACs and internationally. Specifically, graduate and executive courses in international trade, international business, international economics, growth theory and development studies, and so on will find this book relevant.

Acknowledgments

First, in both writing and researching these essays, I benefited enormously from existing literature, individuals, and institutions too vast to even think of listing here. Along the many that deserve mention by name are the following late individuals, from my undergraduate through graduate studies and more, who always, or encouragingly pretended to, like my ideas even when I didn't: George C. Murphy (UCLA), Harland "HP" Padfield (UC Davis and UC Irvine), Emery N. Castle (Oregon State), Michael Rieber (University of Arizona), and my doctoral boss Richard T. Newcomb (University of Arizona).

Second, my editor Joseph Parry at Lexington Books, and his staff, especially Bryndee Ryan and Alison Keefer, have been exceptional. Let me tell a quick story: I first approached Joe about a different manuscript I tentatively called *Selected Reading on the Anthropological Foundations of Economic Behavior, Organization, and Control.* The manuscript was my edited collection of six previously published book chapters by B. Malinowski, M.J. Herskovits, Sir W. Arthur Lewis, Joan V. Robinson, Frank H. Knight, and J. Kornai on economic behavior, economic organization, and economic control. Lexington offered me a contract, and Mr. Parry and I were very excited about bringing the readings to market again in light of economics failure to predict the Great Global Recession of 2007–2010. Only Professor Kornai gracious gave us permission to his essay. The other holders selected to charge exorbitant amounts for their rights, and one in fact republishing their work only months later. I like to think my badgering them motivated republication and the economic literature is no worse off for it.

Third, I am grateful to the anonymous manuscript reviewer for corrections, critical comments, and valuable suggestions. Most of the suggestions are reflected at appropriate places throughout the book; others have opened up wide avenues for future thought and research.

Last, but far not least, I owe a debt of appreciation to my wife and daughter, and I invite all my cheerleaders to share with me the strengths of the book while I absolve them all from any of its weaknesses.

Chapter 1

Introduction

This introduction is a sales pitch for the gains that SSACs made just before the Great Global Recession (GGR) of 2007–2010. This chapter demonstrates that these countries have sufficient capability to reverse their misfortunes and they have done so remarkably in recent years. Whether or not the Great Global Recession (GGR) itself have caused irreparable harm is an interesting and important question, but one that needs a separate analysis. The empirical evidence presented here all points to an SSA that has fared quite well, especially relative to its performance history.

African countries have done relatively well since the mid-1990s. However, little is well understood about how that performance came about. The goal of this book is to enhance the understanding of the recent economic performance of SSACs. To accomplish the goal, I set six manageable objectives and pursue them as the chapters in this book. Empirical and analytical evidence from that pursuit suggests a discernible reversal of misfortunes for these countries. Whether the reversal itself is sustainable (permanent), or the 2008–2010 global recession has already ended the party for these countries are difficult questions to answer. Assuming that SSACs had sufficient capability for good performance before the GGR, even if the recession was a party spoiler, there are at least two things that can be done to revive the party. I outline those issues in the last two chapters, before I conclude.

ECONOMIC PERFORMANCE OF SSACS

In its Summer 1999 issue, the *Journal of Economic Perspectives* (JEP) published a collection of symposium papers on "Slow Growth in Africa." The collection added volume to Africa's literature on the subject.[1] However, the different opinions the papers expressed left a gap in our understanding of Africa's performance. All, but one, JEP papers are generally negative and they paint very different pictures of the same object—Africa. The painting creates an inaccurate impression that Africa's situation is irreversibly hopeless, and that there is nothing anyone can do as these countries cannot even learn from each other. For example, to Paul Collier and Jan Gunning, Africa's performance is a function of external and internal destinies and policies—both permanent curses. Among destinies, the authors include geography and ethnolinguistics. While they stay clear of strong conclusions about the effects of destinies on economic performance, Collier and Gunning clearly conclude that external policies in Africa have improved in recent years, but that domestic policies, especially those relating to private investment, remain the key constraints on economic performance there. Calling out SSACs to own up to their responsibilities rather than blaming external circumstances for their problems is a good thing. Nonetheless, the study fails to acknowledge sufficiently the progress SSACs and other developing countries were making (see, Desai 2008).

In the same collection, Angus Deaton, and Ndulu and O'Connell tell two other stories. Deaton documents a strong relationship between economic growth and historical commodity prices. From that documentation, he concludes that price booms and busts have been important to the economic performance of SSACs. However, the "roots of Africa's slow development almost certainly lie elsewhere, in poor investment appraisal—whether financed from commodity exports or not—and in the quality of governance" (Deaton 1999, 39). Ndulu and O'Connell pick up on the effects of governance on growth in SSACs. Their discussion observes that postcolonial African governments endorsed inward-looking and state-led industrialization policies, and the path they chose simply led them to authoritarianism, fiscal and monetary imbalances, economic decline, and ultimately per capita misfortunes for all their people.

John Sender takes a different tact and a refreshing tone of voice. In reading his piece, one is reminded of Colin M. Turnbull's (1968) *The Lonely African*, whose voice, however loud and clear it might be, is ultimately drowned out by the Africa dilemma itself. The dilemma is not really Sender's, because his critique of the Washington Consensus is crystal clear. He is equally clear about the tragic optimism that development within a capitalist system is an uneven, painful, and costly process that succeeds only when it has domestic political support. The dilemma is that while individually each chapter adds something important to Africa's growth literature, taken together the five pictures the collection paints are astonishingly and irritatingly different to be convincing. Again with the exception of John Sender, the chapters say about SSACs what has always been said about Africa (cf. Stamp 1953;

Junod 1962), and it compares rather peculiarly to contemporary microeconomic evidence (Mahajan 2008; Stiglitz 2010; Fosu 2009; Robinson 2009; Subramanian 2009).[2] For instance, the growth-destiny notion that Collier and Gunning espouse is an old-fashioned fatalism, already available in Andrew M. Kamarck (1976, 1977). Yes, geography is important to economic performance. However, the tropics are a wide area and SSA is not the only tropical region in the world. Thus, while soil fertility is necessary for agricultural productivity, it is not sufficient for the economic performance of many SSACs whose comparative advantages are in the minerals sectors. Indeed, even Kamarck has reconsidered the tropics as a curse per se, because he too acknowledges that the "velocity of change could be harnessed by research" to offset the effects of geography (Kamarck 2000, 235–36).

Similar arguments can be advanced against the claim that SSACs have a higher number of ethnolinguistic groupings than other regions. Of 6,000 or so world languages, only twenty percent (1,200 languages) are African languages. Twenty percent sounds like a lot until one recognizes that three of the major African family of languages are spoken by 400 million people, which means each language group is spoken by 133.3 million people, a number more than the population of any single African country, including the most populous Nigeria.[3] It would seem that the problem is not ethno-linguistics but rather ethno-fragmentation and the lingering effects of the slave trade, both direct results of colonization and colonialism (Rodney 1973; Johnson 1974; Nunn 2008, 2012). As a matter of fact, in South America all ethno-linguistic heterogeneity was eliminated many years ago and replaced by the Spanish and Portuguese languages. Yet, it still remains unclear that language homogeneity reduced ethno-fragmentation or led to economic growth there. Moreover, at its height and prior, the British Empire grew faster than Great Britain in spite of language homogeneity in the latter instance and heterogeneity in the former. One may say that homogeneous South Korea does better than heterogeneous Tanzania, but what is the difference in real performance between Tanzania and Burma, where the latter is more homogeneous than the former?

Available evidence points out that natural resources (including language) are necessary but insufficient growth factors. Indeed, research on the nexus between growth and natural resource continues to produce mixed results; equally resourceful countries have often performed differentially, and some resource-poor nations have indeed done better than their resource-rich counterparts, see, for example, Sachs and Wagner (1999), Rodriguez and Sachs (1999), Auty (1993), and Gylfason and Zoega (2002). Clearly something other than destinies and policies is missing from analysis, and economists would do better searching for the missing link rather than just "translating [their] prejudices into respectable numerals," as E. J. Mishan (1974, 93–94) has charged.

Also unimpressive is the argument that SSACs have had more growth-retarding dictatorships and conflicts. Evidence shows that all African wars and armed conflicts since the 1700s killed fewer than twenty-four percent of the 84.3 million who died in World War II alone. Of 23.4 million people who died in major genocides, ethnic cleansings, and massacres in the period 1939–1945, only 9.12 percent were African, with about sixty-two percent of that taking place in Rwanda, Burundi, and Zanzinbar. War crimes in Africa affected only 5.9454 million people since 1923, an average of 66,060 per annum over ninety years. That number is miniscule compared to 140,000 deaths in the former Yugoslavia over a much shorter time period. The estimated death toll by leader in African from 1885 to 1998 (that including colonial leaders) is only 12.39 million, which pales compared to the 20 million under Stalin in a span of thirty years. Human-caused and aggravated famines and diseases of all recorded time in Africa is only 12.9 percent of those caused by World Wars I and II alone. African riots and political unrests of significance caused only an equivalent of 36.2 percent of the number of people who died during the Hindi-Muslim conflicts in India since 1950 and less than a percent of the two million who perished during the partitioning of India and Pakistan. Only forced labor, slavery, slave trade, and worker abuse present a significant and long-lasting shock. Other conflicts simply measure the weakness or absence of institutions for mitigating conflicts, not the number or severity of conflicts. Hence, the assertion that the South Africa pre-independence in 1994 is the same South Africa post-independence is simply incorrect. In terms of income levels, the old South Africa appears to have outperformed the new South Africa only because the old South African economy excluded the majority of its people. Regarding growth, to those who were excluded even zero growth with inclusion has meant improvement. Thus, generalized cross-sectional emphases of macro-economic variables simply understate the rate of improvement implicit in micro-economic variables. In fact, in reading the historical accounts of the first Europeans to make contact with Southern Africans, like Dr. David Livingstone, for instance, one cannot escape noticing that African countries made unbelievable progress.[4] Wherever one looks, Africa has seen most development in the shortest time period compared to other regions of the world—no question about that! What is interesting (for me) is how African countries developed so much with so little and sporadic economic growth. That assertion represents a fertile research area waiting for intellectual ploughing. Unfortunately Africa is the region where careful studies are rarely carried out. Worse still, and perhaps because of the lack of careful studies, one often hears of the conditions of SSACs inferred from the conditions of other countries, in recent years from the conditions of East Asian countries. In these inferences, observers say of Africa whatever they found to be untrue of other regions. Hence, the "stew" of cross-sectional studies which Ed Leamer (2001) deplores is the worst for African countries, which is a shame because the same experts seem to suggest that Africa needs help the most.

The progress SSACs have made over the years is not discernible because current research often represents Africa by all African poor performers. By contrast, Asia, Europe, and America are almost always defined by the high performers. For instance, in rationalizing the making and essence of the so-called East Asian growth miracles, the World Bank (1993) claims that "from 1965 to 1990 the twenty-three economies of East Asia grew faster than all regions" (1). However, emphasis ends up almost entirely on the eight high-performing economies of Japan, Hong Kong, South Korea, Singapore, Taiwan, Indonesia, Malaysia, and Thailand. How did the rest of the region fare? Would growth have been that spectacular if the poor performers were included? That is an important question to raise because when referring to Africa, the same study excludes Botswana from its discussion on condition that Botswana is a mono-commodity economy. One is then left to wonder what the purpose of comparison in all circumstances is, since nearly all African countries are mono-commodity economies anyway!

I am convinced that by using these arbitrary approaches anyone can just as easily show SSA outperforming other regions in any year; it all depends on which economies one picks to represent that region. If one chooses to represent Africa with Botswana and Asia with Burma, then Africa has grown faster than Asia for more than forty years. If Africa is South Africa (even under Apartheid) and Asia is Afghanistan (even during its calmest years), then Africa is many years more technologically advanced than Asia. Clearly the running of regressions before the data has even been collected seems so wrong (a moral judgment on my part, I know) to continue, but it does continue. Such exercises are a waste of time; they are for the economics profession what IQ debates are for psychology; they generate a lot of interesting information, but little insight. Hence, until researchers begin to study SSACs rather than inferring their situations from other countries, policy-making in Africa will not benefit from recent advances in the economics of growth and technological change.

Take one more example. In an influential IMF paper, Ghura and Hadjimichael (1996) modify Mankiw, Romer, and Weil (1992) to examine the economic growth of a number of SSACs over the period 1981–1992. However, the endogenous aspects of the model motivated in the theoretical part of the paper are ultimately not tested. Hence, the results of the paper lack the prescriptive guts that one would expect from it. Thus, the paper says too much about the poor performance of SSACs and too little about what must be done, and leaves individual countries in the cold (once again). This is a contradiction in terms because unlike purely academic institutions, the IMF and the World Bank's mandates are to support effective policy-making.

TWO THEMES

The usual excuse for the absence of study of SSACs is the lack of data—the false claim that careful studies of African countries are difficult (costly and impossible) to carry out because of the unavailability of data. Despite Yaw Nyarko and William Easterly's (2007) analysis that development is an experimental problem-solving process, and hence "the lacunas in Southern African historical knowledge cannot be attributed to a dearth of data" (Thompson 1969, 3)—, the problem is they are consequences of unfocused research efforts. After all data does not speak for itself in spite of the popular saying. What is needed is understanding rather than knowledge of information, and for that no country has to start from scratch. This means that much of the knowledge required for a decent standard of living anywhere by anyone on earth has already been invented. It is somewhere ready for transfer to where it is needed. The two problems standing in the way are (a) appropriate rules on either side of the transfer channel as Paul Romer (2010) has recently stressed, and (b) lack or limited understanding of knowledge available for transfer.[5] There is no need to reinvent the wheel, and SSACs may finally have found things that make growth work for them.

I exhibit the evidence in two broad themes. The first theme is about the factors and forces behind Africa's recent positive performance. This theme starts with the argument that recent economic performance in Africa has depended upon the intensity of technology use—mainly the newer technologies of internet and mobile (cell) phone. Working silently in support of the intensive use of technology is the technological knowledge of a general nature that has been accumulating over the years in these countries. I demonstrate that fact with annual publications data for Botswana, Namibia, and South Africa for the period 1976–2004. An interesting question that arises is: Why is all this happening now, and is it too little and too late? Part of the answer, it turns out, is external influences like openness and globalization, and the other part is improvement in the quality of local institutions. I show this with two related essays to end the first theme.

The second theme of the book is about how the performance trajectory can be maintained with increasing speed and vitality. If I am correct that the observed reversal of misfortune in SSACs is due to newer technologies made possible by the specialized knowledge that has accumulated over the years, improved quality of institutions, and globalization, then it means in the past the major obstacle to performance was of a technological nature, but it was not the absence of relevant technological innovations! Instead, it was due to inhibited spread of technological innovations (cf. Arrow 1969; Mansfield 1971; Rogers 2003). One obvious inhibitor was the spread of knowledge. The sixth chapter describes some problems with conventional models of the diffusion of innovation and proposes simple modifications. A further obstacle to the diffusion of technological change, which has significant implications for long-run economic growth, is the negligence of resource intra-actions and interactions. Standing on the shoulders of Sir W. Arthur Lewis (1965) and Paul M. Romer (1990, 1993, 1994), I show that resource intra-actions and interactions are important for technological change, and hence for economic growth. Economies with strong positive resource intra- and interactions produce more output than others. In fact, intra- and interactive economies are characterized by economies of scale and would produce twice as much output as others, and their rates of growth and change are high because of it.

CONCLUDING REMARKS

Pre-GGR, the economic performance of SSACs depended on the intensity of use of newer technologies mainly the internet and mobile phone. These technologies are productive because the general knowledge required to make them productive has been accumulating quietly for years. Also over the years, a deeper integration of African countries into the world economy and improving quality of institutions have aided the performance observed since mid-1992. Whether or not the GGR was a "party pooper" for the SSACs is not as important as the fact that these countries can sustain growth, and the spread of technological innovations and intra-active and interactive use of resources remain crucial. The chapters that follow seek to demonstrate this concluding remark.

NOTES

1. In fact, much of this material was written in response to that collection. I shared my comments with Timothy Taylor, Managing Editor of JEP, and I gratefully acknowledge the brief conversation we had.

2. Professor A. Fosu's two volume *Development Success Historical Accounts from More Advanced Countries* (2012), and *Achieving Development Success: Strategies and Lessons from the Developing World* (2013) both by Oxford University Press clarify these issues in a more balanced way.

3. The third largest number of speakers after Indo-European speakers, see *World Fact Book*, Inc., 1999.

4. Henri A. Junod's *The Life of a South African Tribe, Volume II, Mental Life*. University Books, Inc., New Hyde Park, New York, 1962 shows that life was very

different only fifty years ago. To claim that Africa has undergone the least change in the world is just untrue!

5. I am aware of the argument in which the knowledge transfer process is not always Pareto optimal due to resistance to change and other special group self-interests as put forward by Boyan Jovanovic and Yaw Nyarko (1995) in their paper "The transfer of human capital."

Chapter 2

Intensity of Technology Use and Economic Performance

African countries have fared poorly compared to some countries in other regions, but relative to their own performance history some SSACs have done quite well over the recent past. The 1992–2007 decade was especially good, raising the question about how such performance can be made to stick and even expand. This requires better understanding of the source of this good performance, and the current essay, beginning with the assumption that a feeble technology was responsible for slow growth in the past and finds that the impacts of new technologies, measured by the intensities of internet and cell phone use are very strong. The policy implications of the findings recommend increased investment in new technologies for which productivity is high and the adoption and diffusion costs seem low.

African countries suffer from *Africa-itis*—a stigma that makes it hard for observers to notice good economic performance of African countries, and makes it obsessively easy to point out the bad news. As David Bloom and Jeffrey Sachs (1998, 37) put it, it is not only that "Africa surely suffers from a remarkable inattention of the international scientific community," it is also that the little attention that African countries receive is inordinately normative and pessimistic. Rarely do even the best of expert writings on African countries, for example, reveal that although over the 1960–1990 decades African countries made up a large percentage of the "growth disasters," lately some African countries did make it to the list of the "growth miracles" (see Temple 1999, Table 2, 116; Ndulu and O'Connell 1999). During the late 1990s, for example, up to 39 percent of African countries did catch a little of the receding dotcom wave, and many of them grew at rates not lower than two percent per annum, and strong growth continued past 1998. As the dotcom wave subsided, growth slowed to 3.2 percent in 2002, but it climbed back up to 4.3 percent in 2003, 4.6 percent in 2004, and higher still in 2005 (United Nations

Economic Commission for Africa—UNECA 2005). In sum: over the past years to-date African countries have grown at annual rates exceeding four percent, so that by 2004 there were only a few trouble areas in Africa (OECD Observer 2005). Yet, the whole of Africa is more likely to be defined by these few areas than Asia is likely to be characterized by Afghanistan, Pakistan, Burma (Mymar), and North Korea put together.[1]

The cloud of *Africa-itis* is misleading to the extent to which it masks diverse performance across African regions, countries, and even sub-regions within countries, see, for example, IMF (2005). For instance, Botswana and Mauritius have been two of the best performers in the world for nearly four decades. Central African countries have grown at an annual average rate of more than 14 percent during the year 2004–2005. These differences in performance should not be surprising as standard economics teaches that the production possibilities of any economy depend on its technical capability. Technical capability is defined by the quantity and quality of available resources and the current level of technology, so that economic growth is the expansion of production possibilities resulting from improved technical capability, subject to the initial and current institutional conditions, and the policies that govern both. Here is the point: because capabilities differ across economies, so too does economic performance (Amavilah 2006), and no two African should be expected *a priori* to be the same. Yet, too often, analyses of the sources of the economic performance of SSACs focus exclusively either on external factors for which subsequent policy is exogenous, or on some loose generalizations of internal sources of growth for which useful policy is nearly impossible to conduct. For instance, the UNECA study above lists "macro-stability" and "tourism" as the main internal sources of economic performance for Africa in 2004, but then the same report goes on to lament the weak domestic investment, low domestic savings, and the risk of currency appreciation as "some areas of concern." Research must do better than this if it is to serve a credible policy function!

While the quality of resources, such as human capital, which individual SSACs have is a matter of considerable debate, quantitatively most SSACs are no more resource-poor than their counterparts in other regions of the world. For the most part, African countries had colonial experiences not unlike those of other developing countries, suggesting congruent initial conditions across some world regions. Additionally, many developing countries around the world pursued similar economic and political policies immediately upon their political independences, and making similar policy mistakes in the process (Nyarko 2007). For instance, the movements toward resource nationalization and import substitution policies were not unique to African countries. This all seems to imply that observed economic growth rate differences are not principally due to resources, initial conditions, or policy alone.

A reasonable constraint on the economic growth of African countries has been the fact that technological change has never "etherealised" progressively and adequately. This is not a new thesis. Different schools of thought have argued for the fact that it was technological advancement that was responsible for the economic development of industrialized countries, and without innovations, the United States could not have grown, or grown as rapidly. Indeed, the Industrial Revolution set off modern economic growth. However, the new growth theory has brought additional clarity to the understanding that technological advancements are no "manna from the heaven." Technology determines and is determined by economic performance, a joint determination that makes common sense while at the same time raising vexing questions about causality.

For example, a quick glance at the sources of economic growth of the United States over the years would show a clear shift from reliance for growth on resources (Romer's objects) in the early years to healthy interactions and intra-actions of ideas and objects in the middle years, and increasingly to ideas and technology in more recent times (Denison 1967; Gordon 2002; Aghion 2006). Since nothing of the sort has been documented for African countries, it seems reasonable to suspect that a major obstacle to the economic performance of SSACs has been a feeble technological foundation. In dramatic words, just as the craftiest of construction engineers cannot erect a skyscraper on Jell-O pudding, so too strong and sustained growth needs a strong technological foundation.

The objective of this chapter is to quantify some of the technological foundations of economic performance in African countries, using as an example the forty-six African countries listed below.[2] The objective is important because technology improves the productivity of other resources. It is especially crucial where the relative productivity of other factors of production is a matter of considerable concern (Dasgupta and Stoneman 1987). As Aaron Segal (1985) points out "of all gaps that separate Africa from the rest of the world *science and technology is probably the most critical, and the most profound*" (110, italics added). The first section below outlines the theory behind the analysis; the second section turns to practical issues including data, estimations, and results; and the final section makes a concluding remark.

THEORY

This section first sketches the relevant literature and then states a simple and practical model.

Literature

Paul Collier and Jan Willem Gunning (1999) review a very large set of literature on African performance in an attempt to uncover commonalities of the sources of economic performance there. They relate sources of the economic decline of Africa to the lack of social capital, trade openness, public services, financial depth, a hostile geography, and over-dependence on foreign aid. This list is not new; what stands out from this literature review at the aggregate level, however, is the negative effect on performance of the so-called Africa dummy. Consistent with Collier and Gunning, many other researchers report a significant negative African dummy ranging from −0.010 to −0.54 over the decades 1960–1989 (Benhabib and Spiegel 1994; Alcala and Ciccone 2001; Barro 1991; Easterly and Levine 1997). Also during the years 1960–2003, Africa's total factor productivity (TFP) has remained low at between −0.05 and −1.34 according to some estimates (Ndulu and O'Connell 1999; Soderbom and Teal 2003; Jorgenson and Vu 2005).[3] The negative effects of Africa's TFP and dummy are discernible despite the fact that other sources of growth, such as physical capital per worker, or human capital per worker, are not that different from those of other regions.[4]

Temple (1999) looks at the new growth evidence from the perspectives of the old (exogenous) neoclassical and new (endogenous) growth theories. The evidence concludes that differences in economic growth are mainly due to differences in capital investment in equipment, people, and R & D; income inequality and the implication of that for (in-)stability; economic freedom and security of property rights; government and its effects with respect to taxation, spending, regulation, and the financing of infrastructure; and openness to trade. However, Temple's "new evidence" is not really new either; W. Arthur Lewis (1965) argues that "the proximate causes of economic growth are the effort to economize, the accumulation of knowledge, and the accumulation of capital" (164). These causes have strong basis in the quantity and quality of the human population and other natural resources, and in government and government policy. It is not surprising that Temple and Johnson (1998) in associating economic growth with social capability are following Lewis's lead, and here is one insightful sign Lewis posted along the way:

> Economic growth depends both upon technological knowledge about things and living creatures, and upon *social knowledge about man and his relations with his fellowmen.* The former is often emphasized in this context, but the latter is just as important since growth depends as much upon such matters as learning how to administer large scale organizations, or *creating institutions which favour economizing effort*, as it does upon breeding new seeds or learning how to build bigger dams (164; italics added).

The interesting part of this thoughtful line of work is how seemingly noneconomic factors affect the relationship between economic growth and technology (cf. Hoselitz 1952, Fafchamps 2000). This is made clear in a recent paper by Los and Verspagen (2001) which "distinguish[es] four ways in which technology and innovation have their impact on growth" (p. 2). The first channel treats technology either as a pure public good and in that case its rate of change is exogenous, or as a quasi-public good, the rate of which is endogenous. In both cases, technology drives the steady state rate of growth. In turn, technology is a function of factor ratios so that in the exogenous version as the capital-labor ratio increases, the rate of technical change first rises and then falls as diminishing returns to scale set in (Solow 1956, 1957; Swan 1956 [2002]).

In the endogenous version of the model, factor ratios such as the human capital-labor ratio are dynamic with the potential for postponing diminishing marginal products and sustaining convergent/divergent (steady) states (Romer 1989, 1990; Lucas 1988, 1993; cf. Ocampo, Jomo K.S., and Vos 2007). Bennett McCallum (1996) and Mark Rogers (2003) provide excellent reviews of neoclassical exogenous and endogenous growth theories, while Nazrul Islam (2004) assesses the normative (policy) value of endogenous growth theories to developing countries (cf. Stoneman 1987, 154–68).

A second channel is technological diffusion which enables lagging economies to catch up with frontrunners. However, the rate at which economies close the technological gap between them is a function of "social capability" and "technological congruence" (Los and Verspagen 2001). Social capability is the basis for technological "absorptive capability" (Kneller and Stevens 2006), and it has two interactive dimensions: the infrastructural base of which fixed capital such roads, railways, and so on are a major part, and the superstructural base including institutions, social capital, and the like. Technological congruence implies applicability to one country of technology developed elsewhere. This neither dismisses lightly the importance of early arguments about the appropriateness of technology nor overlook a nuanced hypothesis advanced by Yaw Nyarko (2007) of New York University that economic performance is a country-specific problem-solving activity. It does point out, however, the constraining role of rules, and why Paul Romer (2010) is correct in claiming that economic growth in the twenty-first century will depend on trading in rules as opposed to trading in things (Lyons 1987, 169–205).

As third and fourth ways in which technology and innovations enter economic growth, Los and Verspagen point to learning-by-doing (Arrow 1963) and roundabout production (Young 1928). Combined, these two channels permit a demand-driven cumulative impact of technology on economic performance, variously called the Verdoorn-Young-Arrow learning effect, or the Myrdal-Kaldor secular and causal effect (Young 1928; Solow 1997; Arrow 1962, 1969; Kaldor 1966; Thirlwall 1978; Stiglitz 1987, 125–53; Jones and Romer 2010).

Measures of technological capability differ and rank countries differently as Daniele Archibugi and Alberto Coco (2005, 2003) describe (cf. Jeffrey Jones 2006). What is disturbing, however, is that African countries invariably rank low on all key indices of technology. The Technology Achievement

Index (TAI), inspired by the UN Development Programme (UNDP) and outlined in Desai, Fukuda-Parr, Johnson, and Sagasti (2002) focuses on seventy-two countries, dividing them into groups: "leaders," "dynamic adopters," "marginalized," and "others." This index has four dimensions (technology creation, diffusion of new technologies, diffusion of old technologies, and technology relevant human skills). A few African countries on the list score low. African countries are also not doing well on the Technology Index ($Technology_i$ in this essay) assembled by the World Economic Forum. The current essay seeks to understand the effects of technology on per capita real GDP across forty-six African countries in 2004/2005. Such an understanding will help focus the search for the location of the negativity of both the Africa dummy and TFP.

Model

As a starting point, assume a homogeneous Cobb-Douglas technology for the *i*th African country to be

$$Y_i = N_i^{\alpha} K_i^{\beta} \left(Z_i A_i\right)^{1-\alpha-\beta}, \tag{2.1}$$

where Y_i is gross domestic product (GDP), N_i is the population, K_i is the capital stock given by the perpetual inventory formula as net new investment plus old capital stock less depreciation, Z_i is a vector of other output determinants, A_i is the level of technology, and α and β are constant parameters to be estimated. Dividing through by N_i gives (2.1) in logarithmic per capita terms as

$$y_i = \beta k_i + \gamma z_i + a_i, \gamma = \alpha + \beta, \tag{2.2}$$

where $y_i = \ln (Y_i/N_i)$, $k_i = \ln (K_i/N_i)$, $z_i = Z_i/N_i$, and $a_i = \ln A_i$. Subsequent estimations focus on six different versions of (2.2). Next take a look at some practical issues.

PRACTICE

This section describes measurement issues, estimations, and results.

Measurement Issues

The dependent variable y_i is real per capita GDP in US dollars (US$). Chief among independent variables is the capital per capita (k_i)—assuming the rate of labor growth equals that of population. For the lack of data on capital stock, a reasonable measure of k_i is the share of GDP that went to capital formation averaged over the period 2000–2004. The vector matrix z_i includes independent variables such as per capita trade Openness measured as the ratio of per capita exports plus imports to per capita GDP, inflation rate averaged over the years 2000–2004 (ν), and regional dummies for Eastern Africa, Western Africa, Northern Africa, and Southern Africa. Finally, $a_i = y_i - \beta k_i - \gamma z_i$ is a Hicks-neutral productivity shock—a measure of the technological basis of economic performance.

For most countries in this sample, the main data source for y_i are www.earthtends.wri.org and www.finfacts.com. Missing and incomplete data are supplemented by similar data from the International Monetary Fund's (IMF) International Financial Statistics—IFS (2005). Inflation rate (ν) also comes from IFS (2005). The data for Openness, mobile phone (Cellphone), and Internet come from www.Joinafrica.com.

Estimations

I use the OLS estimator of (2) in five fundamental, and four auxiliary versions. In real per capita terms, all nine versions can be generalized to

$$y_i - v_i = a_i + \beta\left[k_i - v_i\right] + \gamma z[_i - v_i] + \varepsilon_i, \varepsilon_i \sim N\left(0, \sigma_i^2\right) \tag{2.3}$$

For example, y_i depends on k_i, Openness, and an index of macroeconomic environment (Macro) in Version1, where the Macro data comes from the World Economic Forum. When Marco data is missing, I use the Africa average Macro (Amacro) variable, calculated as the average sum of available Macro for n countries, that is,

$$AMacro = {}^{1}\!/_{n} \sum Macro_i = 1.78.$$

Version 2 adds to Version 1 Technology$_i$, drawn from Global Competitiveness Reports. Again, where data is missing a proxy was calculated as

$$ATechnology_i = \left[\left(\frac{\sum Technology_i}{2n}\right) - \left(\frac{\sum NRI_i}{2(1-n)}\right)\right] = 1.23,$$

where n are countries for which Technology$_i$ data is available, and 1-n are countries for which Technology$_i$ data is not available, but a partial data series, called Networked Readiness Index (NRI$_i$), is available. For comparison purposes the highest possible score for both Macro and Technology$_i$ is 5.0.

To control for additional variations Version 3 adds regional dummies (Eastern, Western, Northern, and Southern Africa). Version 4 assumes that $Technology_i$ can be decomposed into two components, viz., Cellfone and Internet. The "Internet" variable is the ratio of internet hosts to internet users, and "Cellfone" is per capita cell phones. Both measure the intensity of use of new technologies.[5] Version 5 adds regional dummies to Version 4. Versions 1–5 constitute the fundamental versions of the basic model in (2) or (3). Auxiliary Versions 6–9 are not essential estimations; rather, they are indirect checks on the robustness of the fundamental estimations. For example, Version 6 drops Macro, Version 7 drops Openness, Version 8 drops Internet, and Version 9 excludes Cellfone. The next subsection presents and discusses the results.

Results

Tables 2.1 and 2.2 report estimation results of fundamental and auxiliary versions, respectively. Excluding the constant term the second column of the first table shows, for example, that macroeconomic policy has the largest effect on per capita real GDP across these African countries. Per capita capital and openness to trade are also positively related to per capita real GDP. More than one third of a percentage point increase in y results from a one percentage increase in k (capital) and τ (trade).

A large constant term suggests that some other determinants of real per capita GDP are missing from Version 1. The regression results in the next column of the table add a measure of technology using a technology index calculated by the World Economic Forum (2005). In this case while the coefficients of k_i and Openness remain largely unchanged, the estimate of Macro more than doubles and the constant term falls. A major finding is a huge, negative, and statistically significant impact of technology on the per capita real GDP of these African countries. This implies that the low level of technology harms real income determination in these countries. In fact, the magnitude of this negative coefficient increases significantly when the regression includes regional dummies, suggesting that the sign is not spurious. Southern Africa has the largest regional dummy and Eastern Africa the smallest. With regional dummies included macroeconomic policy becomes even more important than in previous versions. Openness to trade remains positive for GDP, but it is no longer statistically significant.

Columns 4 and 5 of Table 2.1 consider explicit components of technology: the intensity of internet use (Internet) and mobile phone use per capita (Cellphone).[6] Parameters for both variables are large and statistically strong. Such impacts are unaltered by the inclusion of regional dummies, although in this case trade openness becomes insignificant. Even so, the impact of per

Table 2.1 Fundamental Determinants of Per Capita GDP across African Countries, 2004–2005

Variable	*Version 1*	*Version 2*	*Version 3*	*Version 4*	*Version 5*
Constant	4.695 (7.745)	4.153 (7.189)	N/A	5.136 (8.299)	N/A
Investment	0.373 (2.148)	0.357 (2.116)	0.358 (2.387)	0.359 (2.029)	0.368 (1.798)
Openness	0.365 (2.451)	0.362 (2.519)	0.067 (0.548)	0.223 (1.442)	0.099 (0.709)
Macropolicy	0.814 (2.198)	2.396 (4.231)	4.061 (5.519)	0.418 (1.283)	0.292 (1.040)
Technology		−1.169 (−2.68)	−2.621 (−5.03)		
Intensity of Internet Use				5.416 (1.372)	4.829 (1.149)
Intensity of Cellfone Use				3.751 (5.761)	3.316 (4.479)
Eastern Region			3.739 (7.342)		5.094 (8.989)
Western Region			4.268 (8.497)		5.594 (9.233)
Northern Region			4.640 (7.710)		5.849 (8.904)
Southern Region			5.426 (9.843)		
Adj. R^2	0.2126	0.2481	0.5428	0.4325	0.4975
Joint H_0 [*F*]	910.57 [4,42]	763.49 [5,41]	788.39 [8,38]	845.31 [6,40]	637.35 [9,37]
χ^2 (deg.free)	8.273 [4]	1.465 [3]	4.343 [4]	7.515 [2]	6.480 [1]
SEE/Mean	0.1126	0.1100	0.0858	0.0956	0.0899
DW{ρ}	1.904 {0.02}	1.784 {0.07}	1.885 {0.03}	2.454 {−0.23}	2.361 {−0.19}
LLF	−54.972	−53.355	−40.168	−46.318	−41.727

Adj. R^2 = Adjusted R^2, a measure of model explanatory power; *F* = *F*-statistic for joint hypothesis test; Chi-square with degree of freedom, a measure of model goodness-of-fit; SEE/Mean = standard error of the estimate divided by the mean of the dependent variable, a measure of model predictive power; DW = Durbin-Watson statistic for serial correlation; and LLF = Loglikelihood function.

Source: Author's creation.

Table 2.2 Auxiliary Determinants of Per Capita GDP across African Countries, 2004–2005

Variable	*Version 6*	*Version 7*	*Version 8*	*Version 9*
Constant	N/A	N/A	N/A	N/A
Investment	0.406 (2.354)	0.406 (2.155)	0.398 (2.011)	0.342 (1.752)
Openness	0.076 (0.538)		0.067 (0.462)	0.207 (1.476)
Macropolicy		0.246 (0.864)	0.337 (1.209)	0.512 (1.661)
Intensity of Internet Use	5.665 (1.409)	3.659 (0.785)		6.919 (1.246)
Intensity of Cellfone Use	3.470 (4.378)	3.460 (4.631)	3.395 (4.408)	
Eastern region	5.289 (10.355)	5.283 (11.042)	5.120 (8.627)	4.775 (8.401)
Western region	5.796 (10.042)	5.817 (12.311)	5.604 (8.947)	5.327 (9.293)
Northern region	6.282 (9.129)	6.264 (9.853)	6.006 (8.093)	5.818 (8.108)
Southern region	6.052 (9.780)	6.126 (11.69)	5.956 (8.625)	5.780 (8.198)
Adj. R^2	0.5005	0.5041	0.5017	0.3469
Joint H_0 [F]	721.3 [8,38]	726.5 [8,38]	722.9 [8,38]	550.5 [8,38] 3.891 [2]
χ^2 [deg free]	5.061 [2]	6.271 [2]	3.004 [2]	0.1025
SEE/Mean	0.0897	0.0894	0.0895	1.90{0.04}
DW {ρ}	2.47{−0.25}	2.41{−0.22}	2.39{−0.20}	−48.3689
LLF	−42.1994	−42.0370	−42.1483	

Adj. R^2 = Adjusted R^2, a measure of model explanatory power; F = F-statistic for joint hypothesis test; Chi-square with degree of freedom, a measure of model goodness-of-fit; SEE/Mean = standard error of the estimate divided by the mean of the dependent variable, a measure of model predictive power; DW = Durbin-Watson statistic for serial correlation; and LLF = Loglikelihood function.

Source: Author's creation.

capita capital at about 0.37 is robust across all five fundamental versions. The explanatory power ranges from 21 percent to 54 percent, not unreasonable for cross-section regressions and a relatively small sample.

The coefficients of Internet (3.3161) and Cellfone (5.0941) are large. This raises a question about whether or not these variables are overestimated. The results in Table 2.2 indirectly address that concern. For example, Version 6 to Version 9 retain k_i and regional dummy variables as the key independent variables and drop one of the remaining variables from each regression. Version 6 drops Macro; Version 7 excludes Openness, Version 8 leaves out Internet and Version 9 goes without Cellfone. Consequently, there is a remarkable improvement in summary statistics in Table 2.2 compared to Table 2.1; both explanatory and predictive power of the regressions, for instance, increase. However, there is no major gain in the technical efficiency of individual parameters. In addition, the values of the log-likelihood functions decline. This seems to indicate that the fundamental versions in Table 2.1 are more informative than the auxiliary versions in Table 2.2.

CONCLUDING REMARKS

The objective of this essay is to quantify the impact of technology on per capita real GDP of 46 African countries in 2004/2005. The results are encouraging both for policy and further research. The first estimation begins with per capita capital, trade openness, and macroeconomic policy index as the main independent variables, assuming homogeneous technology across countries. These results show that 12 percent of variations in per capita real GDP are explained by those independent variables. A one percentage rise in capital and trade openness contributes more than a third of one percentage increase in GDP, and for macro-policy the effect is three-fourths of a percentage change.

However, the large constant term motivates the inclusion of a country-specific measure of technology. *The negative impact of the technology variable means that technology is a major constraint of the performance of African countries.* This conclusion is consistent with previous observations of a negative total factor productivity (TFP) and or "Africa dummy." Since TFP is a catch-all "measure of our ignorance" (Abramovits 1956), subsequent estimations assess the effects on per capita GDP of the intensity of use of two newer technologies: Internet and Cellphone. Along with the macroeconomic environment, these two variables explain real GDP per capita across countries well. However, there are considerable regional variations.

A number of implications for research and policy emerge from the concluding remark. For instance, the results suggest a need for improved technology.

Increasing the distribution and use of internet and cellphone technologies is one way of doing just that. These new technologies have a good chance of rapid diffusion because "social capability" and "technological congruence" already exist in these countries and the cost of diffusing newer technologies is lower than the cost of adopting and sustaining older technologies. As for further research a key implication of the results is a need to investigate the impacts of old technologies, increasing the sample size, and using alternative modeling and estimations techniques, and better data.

NOTES

1. Kenyan journalist B. Wainaina in "How to Write about Africa I and II" (2005; 2006/2007) argue that there is a standard way people expect about Africa, and unless anyone conforms to that standard, he or she will never be listened to.

2. 1. South Africa, 2. Kenya, 3. Tanzania, 4. Zimbabwe, 5. Mauritius, 6. Cote d'Ivoire, 7. Morocco, 8. Egypt, 9. Mozambique, 10. Namibia, 11. Uganda, 12. Botswana, 13. Zambia, 14. Rwanda, 15. Swaziland, 16. Nigeria, 17. Benin, 18. Democratic Republic of Congo, 19. Madagascar, 20. Senegal, 21. Cameroon, 22. Burkina Faso, 23. Guinea, 24. Tunisia, 25. Sierra Leone, 26. Mali, 27. Togo, 28. Libya, 29. Congo, Republic, 30. Ghana, 31. Malawi, 32. Angola, 33. Ethiopia, 34. Sudan, 35. Burundi, 36. Chad, 37. Somalia, 38. Central African Republic, 39. Lesotho, 40. Gabon, 41. Reunion, 42. Seychelles, 43. Mauritania, 44. Gambia, 45. Cape Verde, 46. Niger.

3. The Africa dummy and Africa TFP are not directly comparable because of different models and estimators. However, the negative signs of the coefficients have been revealingly consistent.

4. Among few exception Kwabena Gyimah-Brempong and Mark Wilson (2005) dispute the Africa differentness.

5. Land-based telephone, railway, and highway intensities were also considered, but dropped because they were multicorrelated with each other and with the capital-labor ratio.

6. Preliminary estimations included land phones, railways, and highways, but there dropped for statistical reason as mentioned above.

Chapter 3

Technology-as-Knowledge and Economic Performance

*This chapter examines annual pooled observations on Botswana, Namibia, and South Africa over the 1976–2004 period to estimate the marginal impacts of technology-as-knowledge on economic performance. It finds that conventional factors of production like capital (*k*), trade openness (*τ*), and government expenditure (*G*) among others, influence economic performance. However, the economic performance of countries like Botswana, Namibia, and South Africa depends largely on technology. For instance, measured as a homogeneous "manna from the heaven," technology is the strongest determinant of real per capita income of the three nations. The strength of such technology as a determinant of performance depends on the knowledge underpinnings of technology (technology-as-knowledge) here measured as the total number of academic publications (*Q*) and discipline-specific number of the same (*q*). Both *Q *and *q *correlate with the countries' performance, which seems to suggest that the "social capability" and "technological congruence" of these countries are improving, and that developing countries like Botswana, Namibia, and South Africa gain from increased investment in knowledge-building activities including publishing.*

The objective of this essay is to estimate the impact of what may be called technology-as-knowledge on the economic performance of SSACs, using limited annual publications data for Botswana, Namibia, and South Africa over the years 1976–2004. The estimation is important for policy and research reasons. For policy, the results informs predictions of long-run economic performance of SSACs like Botswana, Namibia, and South Africa, and other developing countries. Regarding research, it contributes, albeit modestly, to the understanding of the factors and forces that determine economic performance. Such a contribution goes a long way towards opening up opportunities for further examinations of the processes of technical progress and development.

Over the years, growth experts have identified many factors that ostensibly explain the performance of nations, see, for example, Collier and Gunning (1999), Temple (1999), Temple and Johnson (1998), Fafchamps (2004), Barro (1991, 1999), Easterly and Levine (1997), Benhabib and Spiegel (1994), Romer (1993), Artadi and Sala-i-Martin (2003), and Sachs and Warner (1997).[1] In the case of African countries, however, factors undermining growth receive more emphasis than factors promoting growth. W. Easterly and R. Levine (1997), for instance, state that "Africa's growth tragedy" is a consequence of "low schooling, political instability, underdeveloped financial systems, distorted foreign exchange markets, high government deficits, and insufficient infrastructure" (see both the abstract and conclusion of that paper). Their statement may be termed a regression of the negatives, in that both the left-hand side and right-hand side variables are negative and the results appear predictable *a priori*. The opportunity cost of these negative over-emphases is the crowding-out of clarity about the factors that do promote Africa's good performance, which leaves policy-makers scared, but less prepared about what to do. Thus, Kenneth Arrow, in a recent interview with Juan Dubra (2005), is correct that economists still neither understand well the causes of growth, nor do they know why growth rates differ across economies. This situation is not helpful to either policy or further research.

Botswana, Namibia, and South Africa together offer an excellent study example, not because they are located in the same geographical region of the world, but because they represent developing countries in their differences and similarities. In terms of the differences, South Africa is the most technologically advanced of the trio in some respects. However, its nascent democratic institutions and a long Apartheid history have disadvantaged the country in many other important areas. Consequently, South Africa is only an upper-middle-income country. Botswana, on the other hand, has been one of the fastest growing economies in the world for nearly five decades (Acemoglu, Johnson, and Robinson 2001a, 2001b, 2002; Robinson 2009). Rapid performance puts Botswana in the same income category as South Africa. Although Namibia is a lower-middle income country, its modern sectors compares favorably with those of Botswana and South Africa.[2] In some cases Namibia's physical infrastructure is the best in Africa.

With respect to similarities, all three economies are resource-based export economies, with mining (diamond for Botswana, diamond and uranium for Namibia, and precious metals like gold for South Africa) piggybacking each economy for many years. While South Africa's industrial base is the largest of the three, a significant number of people in all these countries depend on domestic subsistence farming for a livelihood. This observation suggests that resource endowment are necessary, but inadequate, conditions for strong industrial growth, an observation not peculiar to developing countries. Relatively resource-poor countries like Finland, or Japan, have done far better than resource-rich countries like the Democratic Republic of Congo. Barbier (2007) made a reasonable case using the United States as an example that natural resource endowment there enables initial growth, but the nexus was not a direct one. Instead, resource endowment generated resource rents (static income), which was then invested in knowledge and technology building. It was the latter two which increased progress. The pathway does not always guarantee success, because resource dependence has led to resource curses and Dutch diseases in some resource-endowed countries (Davies 1995). From Romer's (1986, 1990), we now understand that economies ultimately come to rely increasingly on "ideas" (technology and knowledge) as they become more advanced, implying technological advancements are themselves constrained by knowledge (Amavilah 1996 [1997]), making effective policy an essential argument in economic performance .

The macroeconomic environments and financial sectors of these countries are competitive as well as closely linked as evidenced by the fact that all three nations are members of the Southern African Customs Union within the Rand monetary orbit and the sociopolitical economy of the Southern African Development Community of the proposed African Union (Mshomba 2000, 2009, 2017; Masanjala and Papageorgiou 2006; Aziakpono n.d.; Lange 2004). Consequently, the three countries' going rates of interest and currency exchanges are interconnected. Thus, it is not unreasonable to assume that the level of general knowledge in these countries is approximately the same (World Bank 2001; Marope 2005; Nicolson and Tjezeke n.d.). Moreover, it is also reasonable to say that the prospects for economic integration in this part of Africa is greatest among these three countries. In fact, not long ago the Namibian and South African economies were essentially one economy.

Section 2 below scans the relevant literature for the theoretical insights later used in stating a few empirical relations. Section 3 specifies empirical relations as a simple econometric model with technology-as-knowledge as a key argument. The fourth section describes measurement issues. Section 5 presents the results, and the final section draws a conclusion.

KNOWLEDGE, TECHNOLOGY, PRODUCTION, AND ECONOMIC PERFORMANCE

The role technology plays in the production process, economic performance, and human welfare is no new thing to economists (Arrow 1969; Mansfiled 1971; Sampat 2005, 2006; Rosenberg 1982; Nelson 2002; Mokyr 2005;

Abramovitz 1956, 1979, 1986; Solow 1956, 1957, 1997; Swan 1956 [2002]). This section outlines how knowledge, technology, production, and economic performance relate in literature.

Knowledge and Technology

A key driver of technology is human knowledge and the pretensions about knowledge (von Hayek 1937; Boulding 1966; Loasky 1999; Romer 1989, 1990; Warsh 2006; Brooks 1994). However, although each economy is knowledgeable in its own way, not all knowledge is productive. Moreover, often knowledge may exist but people may not know how use it productively; this is what von Hayek (1974) calls "the pretence of knowledge." Further still, in some economies, productive knowledge is unevenly distributed, and or its rates of growth and spread limited, across the population. This points out that there are institutional factors that influence, not only knowledge accumulation, but also knowledge transfer (Arrow 1969; Jovanovic and Nyarko 1995), and hence their impacts on technology. In fact, long before the endogenous model became a standard tool for accounting performance, Francis Bacon, Adam Smith, Alfred Marshall and so on all have acknowledged the economic value of knowledge in production. For example, common knowledge attributes the saying that "knowledge is power" to Bacon. Adam Smith (1976, 1) argues that the supply of the "necessaries and conveniences of life" depends on the "skill, dexterity, and judgment" of the labor that produces it. For Alfred Marshall, "knowledge is the most powerful engine of production; it enables us to subdue Nature and satisfy our wants" (quoted in Gurak 2004, 1, cf. Amavilah 2009). In this same general area, Bertrand Russel (1948), Thomas Sowell (1996) and many others have stressed the importance of knowledge in different human endeavors, but it is W. Arthur Lewis (1965) who is particularly informative for our purpose.

Lewis ranks knowledge high on his list of "the proximate causes of economic growth," third only after "the will to economize" and "economic institutions" (164). This way of ranking knowledge suggests that a production activity is a function of human effort. A key driver of human effort is the desire for some reward, and the material wealth and comfort, which the reward provides. However, the desire for material wealth in some societies may be limited by such things as "asceticism", social status, and cultural and physical considerations. These limitations suggest either the lack or the weakness of surrounding economic institutions. Where economic institutions are absent, weak, or hostile toward private property rights, the rights to reward work effort and to foster specialization and voluntary exchange of comparative advantages are similarly hampered. Consequently economic freedom is also curtailed, resulting in other institutions such as religion being either too weak, too powerful, or downright destructive.[3] According to Mueller (1983) and Choi (1983), Mancur Olson (1983) has named such a phenomenon "institutional scelerosis," and it happens because economic institutions become dysfunctional (cf. North 1990; Mokyr 2005). Thus, in each society, the growth of knowledge depends on philosophical attitudes, class structure, inventions, and research. The application of knowledge also depends on attitudes to innovations. The idea that norms and value judgments are important to optimizing behavior is a subject of George Akerlof's (2007) "The Missing Motivation in Macroeconomics" (cf. Gunnar Myrdal 1969). Amavilah (2010) has argued that the concept of "control by norms" can be linked to works on economic organization by Knight (1951), Robinson (1970), Lewis (1965), and on the anthropological basis of economic behavior by Herkovits (1952) and Malinowski (1944).

Meadow (1992) defines knowledge as an informative data set known to be true because those who believe it to be true are justified in believing it is true. In order to justify beliefs as true, societies use education to condition beliefs into useful knowledge. Alfred North Whitehead (1929) echoes that notion of knowledge in stating that

> culture is [an] activity of thought, and [a] receptiveness to beauty and humane feeling. . . . [Education] . . . aim[s] at producing men [women] who possess both culture and expert knowledge in some special direction. Their expert knowledge will give them the ground to start from, and their culture will lead them as deep as philosophy and as high as art. [Education should produce useful ideas because], . . . [e]ducation with inert idea is not only useless: it is, above all things, harmful, *Corupti optimi, pessima*. . . . Every intellectual revolution which ever stirred humanity to greatness has been a passionate protest against inert ideas (1–2, [added]).

In contrast to Whitehead and in slight agreement with Meadow, Bertrand Russell (1948, 1953) argues that vague and inexact definitions of knowledge are "inevitable," because "knowledge is a sub-class of true beliefs: every case of knowledge is a case of true beliefs, but not vice versa" (154). In addition, some true beliefs are supported by evidence; they are logical. Other true beliefs need no proof of evidence; they are perceptive and non-logical. Furthermore, Russell considers if it would be sufficient to define knowledge as a self-evident and coherent "whole body of beliefs that promote success" (156). He rejects that definition because "the question 'What do we mean by knowledge' is not one to which there is a definite and unambiguous answer anymore than to the question 'What do we mean by baldness'" (158).

Whereas Russell is vague, Thomas Sowell (1996) is emphatically clear that knowledge and ideas are not the same: "*Ideas are everywhere, but knowledge is rare*" (p. 3, italics added) as not all ideas qualify as knowledge. The few ideas that meet the generality test for knowledge must be produced. The cost of producing knowledge limits the quantity of knowledge available, and one way of cutting the cost of knowledge production is to specialize on the basis of a comparative advantage. That is the supply side of knowledge; the demand side is the notion that the value of the marginal product of knowledge lies in the manner in which knowledge facilitates decision-making. The demand for knowledge is a derived demand as economists would say, and Sowell's book deals with that subject.[4]

Technology and Production

Knowledge is fundamental to technology and hence to economic performance. As Keith Lewin (2006) puts it, "Knowledge matters [a lot] for development." Examples of the influence of knowledge on technology, and vice versa, abound. Driouchi, Azelmad, and Anders (2006) is one recent empirical case. Jared Diamond's (1999) *Guns, Germs, and Steel* is another account, and Carlo Cipolla (1965) is yet another. According to Henderson (1969), the whole Industrial Revolution hinged upon technological progress, and technological progress in turn depends on knowledge (Mokyr 2005; Mansfield 1971). Thus, the seminal studies of human capital such as those by T. W. Schultz (1981) and Gary Becker (1993), and literature reviews like those by Cohn (1979) are all examinations of varieties of knowledge. Although Larry Samuelson (2004) sought a general model for knowledge in economic analysis, most growth studies represent knowledge as education/school and or literacy. These studies are defensible on quantitative grounds; some of them are even groundbreaking. However, knowledge is a lot more than education. Robert Lucas Jr (1993) in his study of East Asian growth miracles conclude that there were really no Asian miracles, and that what has happened is that East Asian economies learned to integrate "objects" and "ideas" in ways that promoted growth (see Romer 1993).

In an incisive chapter, B. J. Loasky (1999) makes clear that observed growth rate differences across economies, insomuch as such differences can be attributed to technological gaps, are essentially "the problem of knowledge" (von Hayek 1937, 1974). To paraphrase, "the problem of knowledge" is due to the incompleteness, uncertainty, and fallibility of information, the complexity of life itself, and the limited absorptive capacity and inability of people to adequately manage change in real time (cf. Kneller and Stevens 2006). Already from Stiglitz (1986, 2000) we know about the problems associated with incomplete, uncertain, and imperfect information. Loasky's new insight is that the uses of knowledge are almost always logical while outputs of knowledge are non-logical, which makes the organization of knowledge into a useful technology very difficult, because technology itself is a complex and multidimensional matrix. Just take one popular definition of technology:

> The entrepreneur's technology is all the technical information about the combination of inputs necessary of the production of output. The production function differs from the technology in that it presupposes technical efficiency and states the *maximum* output obtainable from every possible input combination. The best utilization of any particular input combination is a technical, not economic, problem. The selection of the best input combination for the production of a particular output level depends upon input and output prices and is the subject of economic analysis (Henderson and Quandt, 1980, 66, Italics original).

Although complex, the relationships between knowledge and technology, and technology and production performance are real (see Coelli, Rao, O'Donnell, and Battese 2005). Hence, it is not surprising that Parente and Prescott (1994) argue that economic performance is constrained by barriers to technology. A chief barrier to technology is world knowledge, both general and scientific. The higher the barriers, the lower the level of technology, the more investment in world knowledge is needed to lift economic performance. Using John Kay's (2005) catchy phrase, knowledge can be "big," "small," "precious," as well as base in the sense of Max Lerner (1939).

Production can go on with a given level of technology in the short run as the textbook suggests; in the long run production requires technological change, and change requires knowledge. Joel Mokyr's (2005) description of the history of technology and the effects of technology on long-run economic growth demonstrates that technology presupposes knowledge. For a given level of knowledge, a production activity can be characterized as

$$Y = AX^{\alpha},\ A > 0,\ \alpha > 0, \qquad (3.1)$$

where Y is some output, A is a level of exogenous technology, X are factors of production, and α are the elasticities of X. Then growth accounting models of the general form (3.1), first among them Solow (1957, 1956) and Swan (1956 [2002]), found

$$\frac{\partial Y}{\partial A} > \frac{\partial Y}{\partial X},$$

where the difference, $A = lny - \alpha \ln X \neq 0$, became known as the "Solow/Swan residual" and is a "measure of our ignorance" according to Abramovitz (1956, 1979, 1986) resulting from incomplete specification of X, such as a wrong functional form of (3.1), and or misspecification of X like including wrong, or excluding correct, variables. It made good sense that the missing suspects became entrepreneurship, human capital, and real time. Including these variables allows X to drive A and vice-versa so that (3.1) can be restated as

$$Y = X_i^{\alpha}\left(AX_j\right)^{1-\alpha}, i \neq j, 0 < \alpha < 1. \tag{3.2}$$

Eq. (3.2) gives different perspectives of the role of technology in production. It reveals what Jan Fagerberg (1994) and Fagerberg, Knell, and Srholec (2004) mean when they say that technology gaps explain international growth rate differences. Like in Romer (1989, 1990), they mean A is a function of human capital, implying Y is a function of knowledge. Hence, to say limited technology undermines Africa's economic performance, for instance, is to imply a kind of knowledge deficit there. But technology is a composite knowledge from different sources. JM Keynes (1973) said it well that "part of our knowledge is direct; and part by argument" (p. 3). Since published works are organized arguments, arguments are knowledge, and knowledge is technology. And so, we can argue that for a given level of technology ($A_i(t)$) at time period t a country's measure of economic performance ($Y_i(t)$) depends on it population ($N_i(t)$), its stock of physical capital ($K_i(t)$), its initial conditions as measured by its level of economic performance in year $t = 0$, ($Y_i(0)$), and its other variables ($V_i(t)$), that is,

$$Y_i(t) = A_i(t)N_i^{\alpha}(t)K_i^{\beta}(t)Y_i^{\gamma}(0)V_i^{\delta}(t). \tag{3.3}$$

In recent years international organizations such as the World Economic Forum have constructed indices of policy variables that would fit in V. Unfortunately such data is available only for the most recent years. Two conventional elements of $V_i(t)$ for which data is available are inflation rate ($\Pi_i(t)$) and trade openness ($T_i(t)$). Plugging them into (3.3) we get

$$Y_i(t) = A_i(t)N_i^{\alpha}(t)K_i^{\beta}(t)Y_i^{\gamma}(0)V_i^{\delta}(t)T_i^{\delta_1}(t)Z_i^{\delta_2}(t)\pi_i^{\delta_3}(t), \tag{3.3'}$$

where $Z = V - T - \Pi$. Next we deflate (3.3') by dividing both sides by $\Pi_i(t)$. Further division of the result by $Y_i(0)$ gives real economic performance relative to initial conditions. Dividing (3.3) on both sides by N gives per capita performance as

$$y_i(t) = A_i(t)k_i^{\beta}(t)\tau_i^{\delta_1}(t)z_i^{\delta_2}(t), i = 1,2,3; t = 1,2,3,\ldots, M(t), \tag{3.4}$$

where the lowercase letters are per capita values.

EMPIRICAL SPECIFICATIONS: TECHNOLOGY-AS-KNOWLEDGE AND ECONOMIC PERFORMANCE

To estimate the role of technology-as-knowledge in economic performance we set up a practical econometric model and outline the estimation procedure.

Econometric Model

We specify the econometric model of (3.4) in logarithmic terms as

$$lny_i = lnA_i + \beta \ln k_i + \delta_1 ln\tau_i + \delta_2 lnz_i + \varepsilon_i. \tag{3.5}$$

Then we estimate (3.5) in four broad versions (Version 1, Version 2, Version 3, and Version 4) as a Kmenta-type Cross-sectionally Correlated and Time-wise Autoregressive Model (Kmenta 1986, 622–25; cf. Baltagi 1999). Some versions of (3.5) assume that A_i is homogeneous manna from heaven, while others follow J. Benhabib and M. Spiegel's (1994) account of knowledge (a) as a factor of production, and (b) as a technological force affecting performance through an unspecified Nelson-Phelps channel, because knowledge is more than just an educated labor force alone. Building knowledge is like developing other natural resources. In mining, you discover a mineral ore deposit through investment in exploration. Once ore is discovered you must assay (grade) the ore for quality before developing and mining the property. The quantity of mineral finally recovered depends on all such investments, technology, and market conditions. Knowledge building is the same; *it is mining human population for quality attributes that enhance productivity* (see, Amavilah 2008) Thus, knowledge depends on the "quality of the population" in the sense of Schultz (1981) and Becker (1993). For that reason, we can let

$$A_i(t) = A_i(0)e^{\varphi q_i(t)}, or\ A_i(t) = A_i(0)e^{\varphi ln q_i(t)} \tag{3.6}$$

where $A(0)$ is the initial (year $t = 0$) level of technology, $q_i \supseteq S_i$ is some measure of knowledge, in this case publications, and S_i is a measure of human capital, such as years of schooling in Jones (1997) among many other authors. Then, omitting the time indicator we can restate (3.5) as

$$lny_i = lnA_i + \varphi q_i + \beta \ln k_i + \delta_1 \ln \tau_i + \delta_2 z_i + \varepsilon_i, \tag{3.7a}$$

$$lny_i = lnA_i + \varphi \ln q_i + \beta lnk_i + \delta_1 \tau_i + \delta_2 z_i + \varepsilon_i. \tag{3.7b}$$

Estimation Procedure

The estimation procedure pools together three cross-sections and twenty-nine time-series data into eighty-seven observations. Then we take four distinct steps. The first step assumes the level of technology to be the constant term. The second step introduces "aggregate knowledge" or technology-as-knowledge (Q_i) in the process. The third step disaggregates Q_i into four distinct components: science (q_{i1}), social science (q_{i2}), arts-and-humanities (q_{i3}), and interdisciplinary (q_{i4}), that is, $Q_i = q_{i1} + q_{i2} + q_{i3} + q_{i4}$.

This disaggregation of Q_i assumes that technology-as-knowledge falls into four broad faculties: pure science, pure social science, pure arts-and-humanities, and everything else in between. Hence,

$$y = f(A,X), A = g(q,t), X = h(A,S,t) \Rightarrow y = f(g(h)).$$

Differentiation gives solutions for q, S, and t, with A acting as the variable of integration.

The final step assesses apparent convergence across the three countries, where "convergence" is estimated as,

$$\Delta lny_i = a_0 + a_1 y_i^* = a_2 \Delta \ln q_i + \varepsilon_i, \tag{3.8}$$

for

$$\Delta lny_i = [lny_i(t) - \ln y_i(t-1)], \Delta lnq_i(t) = [lnq_i(t) - lnq_i(t-1)], \textit{and } y_i^*$$

indicates change since 1976 in y of Botswana and Namibia relative to South Africa. Economic performance is "converging" if $a_1 < 0$, and it is converging because knowledge is converging if $a_2 > 0$. Thus, cross-country performance differences narrow with an increased level of economic development as well as with a reduction in the difference of the level of knowledge across economies. This is a significant addition to existing theory, because the opposite is not necessarily true, that is, economic convergence that is not supported by knowledge convergence is not sustainable.

MEASUREMENT ISSUES: VARIABLES, DATA, AND DATA SOURCES

Unless otherwise stated we designate real gross variables with uppercase letters and per capita real variables with lowercase letters, and monetary values are in constant 2000 US dollars and are dated. For example, the dependent variable is gross domestic product (Y, y). For any ith country, (Y, y) depends on its population (N), the rate of investment in physical capital (K, k), and the country's degree of openness to foreign trade (τ). Other independent variables include the ratio of government spending to GDP (G), and the ratio of GNP to GDP (E). G expresses how well government uses public resources. In developing countries governments finance the largest components of human capital building: education and health. A positive impact of G on y would suggest good government policies in a variety of ways (see, for example, Lee 1996 for the case of South Korea). From a negative coefficient one can infer growth-retardant factors associated with the government activity, like corruption, see, for example, Mauro (1995, 1998) and Choi (1983, Chapter 7). E measures the depth of the distribution of income, see, for example, Bertocchi and Canova (1996). A high E represents a large discrepancy between GNP and GDP, reflecting competitive interactions between elements of expropriatory and appropriatory institutions (Acemoglu, Johnson, and Robinson 2002, 2001a, 2001b). That is not necessarily a bad thing; all it says is that a large part of GDP flows out to foreign owners of factors of production.

The data source for y, k, τ, G, and E is the Penn World Table (PWT) 6.2 (Heston, Summers, and Aten 2006). General definitions for these variables are in table 3.1; for technical issues see the PWT Data Appendix and Technical Documentation. The aggregate knowledge variable (Q_i) is "technology-as-knowledge" and equals to the annual number of papers on the ith country: $Q_i = q_{i1} + q_{i2} + q_{i3} + q_{i4}$, where q_{i1} represents science papers, q_{i2} represents social science papers, q_{13} is for arts-and-humanities papers, and q_{i4} are interdisciplinary papers. The latter came about because in some cases $Q_i \neq \sum_{i=1}^{T=4} q_i$, which means that some papers counted more or less than once. Since knowledge is cumulative, this variable performs a function similar to an interaction term. The data source for (Q, q) is Thomson Scientific (2006).

We assume that z is a country specific dummy variable of unspecified dimensions. It is defined as the number of years since a country attained its political independence. For example, in 1976, Botswana, Namibia, and South Africa had been independent for 10 years, −14 years, and −18 years, respectively. By 2004, Botswana was thirty-nine years old, Namibia was fifteen, and South Africa only eleven. The coefficient of this variable captures the impacts of factors like political freedom and democracy (Levine 1995; Perssons 2005; Schumpeter 1950; Landes 1998). In addition, the level of economic development (y^*) is important; it captures the difference in the level of economic activity for Botswana and Namibia relative to South Africa, taking the initial year (1976) as the base, that is,

$$y_i^*(t) = \frac{\left[y_{sa}(t) - y_i(t)\right]}{y_{sa}(0) - y_i(0)}, 0 < y_i^*(t) \leq 1, \tag{3.9}$$
$$i = Botswana,\ Namibia,\ sa = South\ Africa,$$

where the numerator is the difference in the level of development between the *i*th economy and South Africa in the *t*th year and the denominator is the difference in the same in the initial year ($t = 0$).

Then relative to its own level of development in 1976, the level of development of the South African economy in the tth year becomes

$$y^*_{sa}(t) \equiv y^*_i(t) = \left[y_{sa}(0) + y_{sa}(t)\right] / y_{sa}(0) = \left[1 + y_{sa}(t) / y_{sa}(0)\right] \quad (3.10)$$

The coefficient on y^* is essentially the relative coefficient of "convergence," similar, but not identical, to the so-called catch-up effect.

RESULTS

Assuming a homogeneous level of technology (A), the initial estimations show that only G has a positive coefficient, and the constant term (lnA = 9.822) is very large. By letting A be some linear function of Q and a random error term (μ), that is, $A = aQ + \mu$, the results show that one publication adds seventeen cents ($0.17) to per capita income, while an increase of one dollar in G has the effect of raising real GDP per capita by about thirty-nine cents (US$0.39). The conventional variables, k and τ, contribute very little to income per capita in this case. In fact, an increase of one percentage point in k reduces y by 0.6 percent, whereas the contribution of τ is only slightly over 1 percent (1.2%).

Disaggregating Q, we find that

$$\frac{\partial lny}{\partial \ln q_1} > \frac{\partial \ln y}{\partial\partial \ln q_3} > \frac{\partial \ln y}{\partial \ln q_2} > \frac{\partial \ln y}{\partial \ln q_4}.$$

Consequently, although the inclusion of Q and its parts improved the generalized explanatory power measured by the Buse R-square, parameter estimates remained technically inefficient, and the constant term stayed above the mean of the dependent variable (8.6452). The very low Durbin-Watson statistics indicate serial correlation, motivating the inclusion of the lagged y, $y(t\text{-}1)$. However, the inclusion of $y(t\text{-}1)$ merely redistributes the weights of the variables, and the size of the intercept does not change much. In addition, τ now has a negative sign and k a positive one, and both are statistically insignificant. The short run impacts of Q and its components are statistically strong. Econometric adjustments such as dropping all insignificant variables, do not resolve these problems of insignificance and incorrect signs elsewhere.

While the statistical significance is troubling, the substance of the results is reasonable. For instance, Tables 3.1–3.5 reveal that technology explains

Table 3.1 Key Variables and Data Sources

Description	*Symbol*	*Data Source*
Real per capita GDP, chained	y	PWT 6.2
Investment/GPD ratio	k	PWT 6.2
Openness=(total trade/GDP ratio)	τ	PWT 6.2
Knowledge = Annual publications	Q	Thomsom Scientific
• Science publications	q_1	
• Social Science publications	q_2	
• Arts-n-Humanities publications	q_3	
• Interactions = interdisciplinary publications	q_4	
Years since independence	z	Own calculations
Level of development	y^*	Own calculations
Government share of GDP	G	PWT 6.2
Penetration of income (GNP/GDP ratio)	E	PWT 6.2

Source: Author's creation.

much of the observed variations in per capita income of developing countries like Botswana, Namibia, and South Africa. Particularly Tables 3.4 and 3.5 derive from the idea that the level of technology (A) has at least three components: one due to random error (μ_A), the second due to economic efficiency (A_E), and the third to technological progress (A_T), that is, $A = A_E + A_T + \mu_A$.[5]

Table 3.2 Determinants of Real GDP Per Capita, Botswana, Namibia, and South Africa, 1976–2004[a]

Variable	*Version 1*	*Version 2*	*Version 3*
Constant ≡ A	9.8256 (29.811)	8.9400 (10.212)	8.6958 (7.9459)
Investment-GDP ≡ k	−0.0238 (−0.8615)	−0.0069 (−0.1741)	0.0085 (0.1889)
Openness ≡ τ	−0.155 (−3.5695)	0.0127 (0.1564)	−0.0123 (−0.2821)
Country dummy ≡ z	−0.0102 (−0.5243)	−0.0392 (−2.132)	−0.0357 (−1.6767)
Knowledge ≡ Q		0.16871 (6.7452)	
Science ≡ q_1			0.0705 (2.8791)
Social Science ≡ q_2			0.0369 (1.0895)
ArtsHumanities≡q_3			0.0541 (2.8904)
Government ≡ G	0.0099 (0.1586)	0.3738 (5.2973)	0.5468 (6.7005)
GNP/GDP ≡ E			−0.4157 (−1.8615)
Dev. Level≡ y^*			−0.446 (−7.7990)
Buse R^2	0.3811	0.6722	0.7469
Buse Raw Moment R^2	0.9994	0.9997	0.9997
SEE	0.93004	0.98468	0.98154
LLF	−634.802	−651.534	−658.455
DW [ρ]	0.7288 [0.4266]	0.8878 [0.4233]	1.0054 [0.3964]
Normal t	−4.4934	−3.5580	−3.5210

SEE = standard error of the estimate; LLF = Loglikelihood function; DW = Durbin-Watson statistic for serial correlation; and Dev. Level is level of the country's development.

Source: Author's creation.

[a]Parentheses are t-ratios at the 5 percent significance level. Square brackets are ρ statistics.

Table 3.3 Determinants of Real GDP Per Capita, Botswana, Namibia, and South Africa, 1976–2004[a]

Variable	*Version 1*	*Version 2*	*Version 3*
Constant ≡ A	9.1904 (22.772)	8.5532 (9.2562)	8.4442 (7.9104)
Lagged $y \equiv y(t\text{-}1)$	0.0561 (4.5037)	0.0378 (3.1050)	0.0393 (3.0692)
Investment-GDP ≡ k	−0.0726 (−1.9226)	−0.0249 (−0.5986)	−0.0175 (−0.3959)
Openness ≡ τ	−0.3031 (−4.7405)	0.0056 (0.0631)	−0.0772 (−0.9179)
Country dummy≡ z	−0.0361 (−1.4721)	−0.0377 (−1.9627)	−0.0358 (−1.7195)
Knowledge ≡ Q		0.1462 (5.2449)	
Science ≡ q_1			0.0539 (2.2406)
Social Science ≡ q_2			0.0406 (1.1916)
Arts Humanities≡ q_3			0.0487 (2.4173)
Interactions ≡ q_4			−0.0137 (−0.6716)
Government ≡ G	0.2579 (3.3472)	0.4060 (5.8318)	0.4955 (5.9521)
GNP/GDP ≡ E		−0.3927 (−1.8963)	−0.3102 (−1.4147)
Dev. Level ≡ y^*	−0.3729 (−6.3728)	−0.3953 (−7.9163)	−0.4345 (−8.1348)
Buse R^2	0.6061	0.7415	0.7787
Buse Raw Moment R^2	0.9992	0.9997	0.9996
SEE	096611	0.98007	0.97751
LLF	−653.334	−649.845	−654.109
DW [ρ]	0.8025 [0.5534]	0.9735 [0.4491]	1.0536 [0.4214]
Durbin H	5.1974	4.2192	3.9589
Normal t	−5.2635	−3.9837	−3.5396

SEE = standard error of the estimate; and LLF = Loglikelihood function.
Source: Author's creation.
[a]Parentheses are t-ratios at the 5 percent significance level. Square brackets are ρ statistics.

Table 3.4 Determinants of Real GDP Per Capita, Botswana, Namibia, and South Africa, 1976–2004

Variable	*Version 1*	*Version 2*	*Version 3*
Investment-GDP ≡ k	0.0983 (1.3790)	0.1521 (2.3186)	0.2535 (3.2649)
Openness ≡ τ	0.9107 (9.4286)	1.0001 (11.278)	0.9211 (8.1097)
Country dummy≡ z	0.1790 (4.1697)	−0.0588 (−1.6242)	−0.0628 (−1.5844)
Knowledge ≡ Q		0.4377 (14.071)	
Science ≡ q_1			0.2029 (5.1040)
Arts Humanities ≡ q_3			0.2008 (6.4849)
Government ≡ G	1.1837 (10.983)	0.6625 (5.7213)	0.9654 (7.0086)
Dev. Level ≡ y^*	−0.4206 (−4.042)	−0.5274 (−6.1234)	−0.6087 (−7.1971)
Buse R^2	0.2300	0.2328	0.5916
Buse Raw Moment R^2	0.9979	0.9978	0.9988
SEE	0.99378	0.98901	0.98822
LLF	−710.675	−696.394	−711.556
DW [ρ]	1.7717 [0.40165]	1.5063 [0.1771]	1.5428 [0.1688]
Normal t	−0.5580	−0.9158	−1.3924

SEE = standard error of the estimate; LLF = Loglikelihood function; and DW = Durbin-Watson statistic.
Source: Author's creation.

Table 3.5 Determinants of Real GDP Per Capita, Botswana, Namibia, and South Africa, 1976–2004

Variable	*Version 3.1*	*Version 3.2*
Lagged $y \equiv y(t\text{-}1)$	0.0599 (2.9267)	0.0349 (1.7470)
Investment-GDP $\equiv k$	0.0686 (0.9287)	0.2276 (2.9562)
Openness $\equiv \tau$	0.7751 (8.0086)	0.9241 (8.2368)
Country dummy $\equiv z$	0.1903 (4.0998)	−0.0571 (−1.4628)
Knowledge $\equiv Q$		
Science $\equiv q_1$		0.2012 (5.1530)
Arts Humanities $\equiv q_3$		0.1886 (5.8699)
Government $\equiv G$	1.2276 (11.899)	0.8893 (6.2865)
Development Level $\equiv y^*$	−0.3942 (−3.5704)	−0.0349 (−6.8540)
Buse R^2	0.910	0.6203
Buse Raw Moment R^2	0.98948	0.9988
Std. Error Estimate	0.99473	0.98422
Loglikelihood Function	−707.542	−710.687
DW [ρ]	1.7223 [0.0305]	1.5555 [0.1488]
Durbin *H*	0.29033	1.1423
Normal *t*	−0.4436	−1.8323

Source: Author's creation.

This explains why adding Q to the regression reduced *A* somewhat although it remains above the mean of the dependent variable. The marginal impact of a publication on *y* remained roughly the same at sixteen cents (US$0.155). Disaggregating Q into science (q_1), social science (q_2), arts-n-humanities (q_3), and an interdisciplinary term (q_4), considerably improved the explanatory power of the regressions.

Three findings stand out from this. First, the time elapse since independence (*z*) has a negative partial coefficient, which is understandable. By 2004 Botswana had been independent for more than three decades. Interpreted as a measure of democracy, economic freedom, the rule of law, historical legacies, and so on, the negative sign on *z* is consistent with increasing evidence of negative impacts of historical legacies on performance (Nunn 2005, 2004; Nunn and Puga 2012; Bertocchi and Canova 1996; Masanjala and Papageorgiu, undated, Lange 2004). In this respect, Namibia and South Africa have not even begun to recover from their historical hangovers, which weighs down the average performance for the three nations. Also negative is the impact of economic penetration (*E*). For each one dollar's worth of an increase in this ratio, 40 cents' worth of *y* is lost to foreign owners of productive resources. In this case the result captures the extractive nature of these three economies.

Likewise, Botswana and Namibia have closed the absolute gap in the level of economic development between them and South Africa, that is, income increases as the gap narrows. However, the relative gap persists. For instance, Botswana's *y* has converged to that of South Africa more than Namibia's has, which makes sense because Namibia and South Africa started off more similar and are now barely converging, if not diverging, as each country attempts to assert its political independence. South Africa has not progressed a lot past its 1976 level. This too is to be expected; prior to independence in 1994, most black South Africans were excluded from the modern accounting of the economy and so *y* was overstated. The end of Apartheid meant the inclusion of many more people in the economy, and so *y* fell.

The results are unchanged when $y(t\text{-}1)$ is included. Notable from the tables is that the effects of aggregate *Q* on *y* lie between \$0.014 and \$0.017, while those of disaggregate *Q* range from US\$0.03 to US\$0.07. In all this q_2 has the weakest effect on *y* at the 5 percent significance level. These findings are encouraging, although the wrong (or sometimes switching) signs on the key variables *k* and τ are troubling. How can these results be corrected?

Again, Tables 3.4 and 3.5 present results from estimations that set the constant term to zero. As is the usual case with "noconstant" regressions, and in this case given that our pooled series has more time-series than cross-sections, the "generalized proportion of variations" (Buse *R*-square) in *y* that is explained by the included variables is reasonable; it ranges from 23 percent to 78 percent—not bad at all, because it is possible for an *R*-square to be negative in situations like this one. What is important is that now the coefficients on both *k* and τ are positive and statistically significant at the 5 percent level. The marginal impact of technology as knowledge in the aggregate (*Q*) or in the disaggregate (*q*) is also positively strong, especially for q_1 and q_3.

Table 3.6 presents tentative results for the estimation of (3.8). These are apparent, rather than convergence as precisely defined and measured according to Mankiw, Romer, and Weil (1992) and the subsequent literature such as Islam (1995), Higgins, Levy, and Young (2006), and Jones (1997, 2002). But the estimates are consistent with Bernard and Jones (1995) in establishing the link between *Q* and *q* on one side and *y* on the other side. In this link the contribution of science publications is the strongest, and the level of development is also essential.

CONCLUDING REMARKS

What do we conclude from the results, and what are the implications of the conclusion for policy and further research? The examination agrees with Robert Barro's (1991) conclusion that regression analyses often leave unexplained factors that determine the economic performance of developing

Table 3.6 Apparent Convergence across Botswana, Namibia, and South Africa, 1976–2004. (Uncorrected and corrected results with a constant term, Parentheses are t-ratios at 5 percent significance level)

Variable	*1a*	*1b*	*2a*	*2b*
Constant $\equiv a_0$	−0.0227 (−0.2222)	−0.045 (−0.8938)	−0.1179 (−0.8849)	−0959 (−0.7424)
y^*	−0.0155 (−0.1739)		0.1704 (1.2104)	0.1398 (1.0504)
ΔlnQ	0.9065 (14.120)	0.9017 (14.042)		
Δlnq1			0.2232 (3.1491)	0.2241 (3.1661)
Δlnq2			0.6225 (6.6214)	0.6341 (6.898)
Δlnq3			0.0696 (0.6834)	−0.1196
Δlnq4			−0.1535 (−1.7455)	(−1.6637)
Buse R^2	0.7236	0.7201	0.6160	0.6120
Buse MomentR^2	0.7243	0.7206	0.6271	0.6232
SEE	0.3597	0.9385	0.88104	0.88422
LLF	−61.916	−61.6287	−62.5298	−62.8197
DW[ρ]	1.2483 [0.1562]	1.2476 [0.1577]	1.2668 [0.09477]	1.2542 [0.10525]

SEE = standard error of the estimate; and LLF = loglikelihood function.
Source: Author's creation.

Table 3.7 Apparent Convergence across Botswana, Namibia, and South Africa, 1976–2004. (Uncorrected and corrected results without a constant term, Parentheses are t-ratios at 5 percent significance level)

Variable	*1a*	*1b*	*2a*	*2b*
y^*	−0.0329 (−0.7900)		0.0452 (0.9251)	0.0391 (0.84138)
ΔlnQ	0.9043 (14.098)	0.8970 (14.026)		
Δlnq1			0.1897 (2.7211)	0.1904 (2.7656)
Δlnq2			0.6007 (6.5374)	0.6073 (6.9446
Δlnq3			0.0459 (0.4551)	−0.0841 (−1.261)
Δlnq4			−0.1048 (−1.308)	
Buse R^2	0.7222	0.7138	0.5909	0.5908
Buse Moment R^2	0.7230	0.7141	0.6007	0.6007
SEE/Mean	0.88422	0.9514	0.8686	0.87325
LLF	−6.8197	−62.1361	−61.3310	−61.5015
DW[ρ]	1.2542 [0.1025]	1.2200 [0.1759]	1.2815 [0.06911]	1.2853 [0.07195]

SEE = standard error of the estimate; and LLF = loglikelihood function.
Source: Author's creation.

countries. Primary factors such as capital, and secondary or higher resources like trade, and *G*, are important to economic performance. Even so, a more persuasive case than the factors of production is that the economic performance of countries like Botswana, Namibia, and South Africa depends increasingly on a combination of technology and knowledge, which I have called "technology-as-knowledge" in this essay. Measured as a homogenous 'manna from heaven," technology is the strongest determinant of *y* in Botswana, Namibia, and South Africa. What is going on in the black-box can in fact be explained by technology-as-knowledge, represented by aggregate *Q* and disaggregate *q* number of publications. Both *Q* and *q* are strongly correlated with the three countries' economic performance. More precisely the economic performance of these nations benefits most from science (q_1) and arts-n-humanities publications (q_3). Social science (q_2) publications have a positive but statistically insignificant effect on *y*.

The positive effect of science on *y* supports the notion of the increasing "social capability" of these countries. The strong correlation between arts-n-humanities and *y* signals improving "technological congruence" along with enhanced absorptive capacity. These assertions require further research. What is clear now is that the positive, but weak, effect of social science on economic performance is a reflection of an excess supply of publications in this area, as well as associated deadweight losses as evident from the low marginal impacts.

The policy implication of the conclusion is that developing countries like Botswana, Namibia, and South Africa would gain from increased investment in knowledge-building activities including publishing—a paper is worth more than its light weight, so to speak. This potential gain justifies further research on the topic. For example, one may enlarge the sample size, and explore better and richer sets of data than those utilized here. Another attempt may deploy alternative estimators and estimation techniques. A third, may use sophisticated functional forms which might yield better results than we have here. However, despite their limitations, the results of this analysis are encouraging.

NOTES

1. I list only a few examples among many; for a long list go to http://ideas.repec.org/g/afrogro.html.

2. Income groups: according to the World Bank's Atlas method in 2005, low-middle-income economies are those with an annual gross national income per capita of US$875 or less; lower-middle-income ranges from US$876–US$3,465;

upper-middle-income lies between US$3,466 and US$10, 725; and high income is US$10,726 and above.

3. Lewis's definition of "economic organization" is that of Frank Knight (1921).

4. Charrtrand (2002, 2006) has assembled a searchable database containing over 1,000 papers on the global technological competitiveness of knowledge-based economies.

5. Amavilah (1997; 1996, 77–80) outlines this idea.

Chapter 4

Resources, Governance, and Global Links and Economic Performance

This chapter shows that the economic performance of a group of thirty-eight African countries in 2000, 2002, and 2007 depended on three broad sources: domestic resources, governance, and global links. The results reveal that investment in physical capital plays the most important part. The effects of education as a component of human capital are modest, while those of the health part of human capital are negative. At the aggregate level, external relations are positively correlated with per capita income. However, disaggregated as integration, aid dependency, and net tourism, all three global links have a negative effect on performance. Also, two indicators of institutional quality (governance) show that average improvement in the quality of institutions has helped economic performance. Considering different dimensions of institutions, the rule of law and the safety and security of property rights are the most constraining aspects of institutions on economic performance in this group of countries. The findings leave enough room for technical fine-tuning and sophisticated estimators, which cautions interpretation. However, it seems clear that developing countries do better improving domestic resources and institutions than relying for performance on external relations, even though such links are important as well.

In recent years, especially just before the GGR and anti-government uprisings in North Africa and the Ivory Coast, SSACs have fared well relative to their performance history. Continent-wide, during those years, only the HIV/AIDS problem represented a unique and present danger. Individually, even traditional laggards, corruption-laden and coup-prone nations have done well on the economic front. This performance has prompted Jorge Arbache, Delfin Go, and John Page (2008) to ask whether "Africa's economy is at a turning point." What explains the recent performance, and how can it be made to stick? The preceding two chapters argued for intensity of technology use and technological knowledge. This chapter broadens the scope to estimate and comment on the effects on economic performance of key domestic resources, governance as a measure of institutional quality, and international relations (global links) across thirty-eight SSACs in 2000, 2002, and 2007. The exercise is important for understanding the relative significance of the sources of economic performance for a region that has until recently suffered one misfortune upon another. The inspiration is the beautiful structure of the World Bank's World Development Indicators (WDI) reports, which suggest that economic performance of any country depends on its people, its environment, its economy, its current technological and market states, and its international relations (see any WDI copy). From this inspiration, the analysis relies on simple rules of inference of a conventional production function. Despite their simplicity, the transformations are powerful enough for the purpose at hand.[1]

Here is how the exercise proceeds. The next section scans the literature in search of the theoretical foundations of the estimations. The third section states the analytical framework, while the fourth section describes the estimations themselves. The results and their implications come in the fifth section, followed by a concluding remark in the last section.

SOURCES OF RECENT ECONOMIC PERFORMANCE

The recent economic performance of SSACs came from three broad sources: (a) domestic resources (factors and forces of production), (b) governance (a measure of institutional quality), and (c) global links (measures of openness to external contacts).

Economic performance and domestic resources

Economic performance and primary factors of production

The vast literature on the primary sources of economic performance is now well understood. Pre-independence growth was an extensive type of growth deriving from the growth of labor, land (mainly mineral and agricultural commodities), fixed physical capital in agriculture, and in mining and quarrying (see Fafchamps 2000; Amavilah 1996). In fact, W. Arthur Lewis (1954) sought to explain how such growth might be sustained with his now classic paper "Economic Development with Unlimited Supplies of Labour."

Post-independence Tahari, Ghura, Akitoby, and Aka (2004) find that for SSACs growth during the 1960–2002 years depended on the accumulation of "objects" rather than "ideas"—to use Paul Romer's (1993) lingo (cf. Ndulu and O'Connell 1999). Over the same time period, only Botswana, Equatorial

Guinea, Gambia, and Mauritius grew at rates exceeding four percent per annum (Basu, Calamitsis, and Ghura 2000; Acemoglu, Johnson, and Robinson 2001a). Overall capital accumulation contributed to growth more than labor, although Amavilah (1996, 1998) suspects double-counting as a result of recording improvements in mining, for example, as additions to both primary sector and secondary sector capital. Beginning c. 1997, the number of SSACs with growth rates above 4 percent more than doubled.[2] What explains this turnaround of things?

Economic performance and secondary or higher resources

By secondary or higher resources, I mean "fluid capital" and human capital.[3] According to Taylor (2000), fluid capital is cumulative net investment plus allowable depreciation (cf. Amavilah and Newcomb 2004). Net investment is subject to the *capacity to invest* for which the limit is set by the financial system (money economy). Depreciation is conditional on in-situ *capacity to produce* determined by the real economy. Regarding human capital, Tahari, Ghura, Akitoby, and Aka (2004) argue that the recent growth of SSACs is due to improved institutional quality, improved macroeconomic policy environment, and the broadening of the export base from a narrow range of commodities to semi-processed goods. A preceding essay presents evidence supporting the positive effects of macroeconomic policy on the performance of forty-six African countries in 2004. These changes facilitated human capital accumulation. What seems relevant to point out is that Stephen O'Connell and Benno Ndulu (2000), and Ndulu and O'Connell (1999) associate the performance of SSACs with capital accumulation, demographic changes, policy, institutions, political (in)stabiliy, and total factor productivity (TFP), where TFP is proxied by the number of years of schooling. In that sense, TFP is the same thing as human capital (*H*). Drawing on Barro and Lee (1993, 1996, 2000), dataset for the value of human capital in economic performance, Benhabib and Spiegel (1994) also show that most African countries lack the critical mass of *H* stock required for fast-growing.

Economic performance and forces of production

From both W. Arthur Lewis (1965) and Paul Romer (1990, 1993, 1994), economic performance depends on factors and forces. A number of forces underscore the performance of SSACs. Key among them are technology and institutions, where technology is measured variously as TFP and or Solow residual (*A*). Institutions are often proxied by governance. Because of poor governance, in a recent paper, Jean-Claude Maswana (2006) associates poor performance of African countries with lack of technological innovation and its underlying knowledge, and bad policies. Thus, the significance of institutions for economic performance has never been an issue for debate. The controversy has been over how to quantify the role of institutions.

Economic performance and governance

The extant literature shows that conventional factors and forces of production are necessary, but not enough to explain economic performance. Increasing evidence points to institutions and institutional quality as essential elements in the growth of both output, resources, and resource productivity. This is, however, not new evidence as classical economists like Adam Smith (1973 [1776]), new classical economists like W. Arthur Lewis (1965), contemporary theorists like North (1990), and others like Gradstein and Konrad (2006), to mention a few randomly, all touch upon the role in economic performance of institutions and institutional quality. Aron (2000, Table 1, 108–113) provides an excellent review of the links between institutions and the economic performance of developing countries. From the review it is clear that countries with "good" institutions tend to do better than countries without or with "bad" institutions. What remains controversial is how to quantify the effects of institutions, but even that concern is fast waning, given what we now know from Acemoglu, Johnson, and Robinson (2001b, 2002), Nunn (2008, 2005, 2004), Acemoglu and Johnson (2007), Amavilah (2006), and many others. In fact, some experts, like Sachs and Warner (1997), and Bloom and Sachs (1998) use geography to describe institutional effects on growth. Others turn to proxies like constitutions, political freedoms and social justice. Nunn and Puga (2012) have added "ruggedness" to capture the combined effects of geography and institutions implied by the slave trade. In the past, African countries have not done well by such measures, and it is worthwhile taking another look.

Among other measures of institutional quality, governance has been the preferred indicator. For this reason subject experts collect, rationalize, and update data for what now is called the Kaufman- Kraay-Zoido-Mastrzzi (KKZM) index of governance (Kaufman and Kraay 2008). Quibria (2006, 104), for example, shows that the KKZM composite correlates positively with the economic growth of a number of Asian countries. Of the eighteen or so common indices of governance, the World Bank's Worldwide Governance Indicators (WGI) are the most comprehensive. WGI covers 212 countries and territories over 1996–2006, and it has six dimensions: (a) voice and accountability, (b) political stability and absence of violence, (c) government and effectiveness, (d) regulatory quality, (e) rule of law, and (f) control of corruption. All six dimensions, individually and collectively, say something important about economic performance. For instance, where the rule of law is absent or weak, property rights will be fragile, markets dysfunctional, and economic performance most likely unsustainable.

In October 2006, the Mo Ibrahim Foundation, then at Harvard University's Kennedy School of Government, released its own Mo Ibrahim African Governance Index (MIGI). Based on 2005 data, MIGI expands on a similar series for 2000 and 2002, and covers forty-eight countries, and the MIGI governance data of the thirty-eight countries in this essay come from here. The compilers and financier of the MIGI claim that it is geographically more comprehensive than similar indices, and addresses the biases that afflicted competing indicators like the WGI.

Economic performance and global links

Countries no longer operate in isolation no matter their size and economic conditions. External relations play a role in the performance of nations, and the debate about the merits and demerits of globalization centers around this issue. For instance, for a long time research has shown a strong correlation between foreign trade and economic growth (see Frankel and Romer 1999). In fact, different versions of trade-led growth were popular in the 1970–1980s (Choi 1983, Chapters 5 and 6). There are doubtful questions about the effects of foreign assistance on economic performance of developing countries, with some putting it down and others advocating at least "aid for trade" (Moyo 2009). However, the fact that these countries want aid increased suggests that aid is important at least for some countries and some needs (Sssozi, Asongu, and Amavilah 2017). And there are pertinent issues of international finance, especially debt and debt servicing (Ndikumana and Boyce, 2011), and the handling of trade disputes at the WTO (Mshomba 2009). There is thus a need for economic models to allow for global links, and I suggest one next below.

ANALYTICAL FRAMEWORK

The value of the ith country's economic activity, such as its gross domestic product (Y_i) depends on the country's technical capability (X_i), that is,

$$Y_i = F\left(X_i\right), i = 1,2,3,\ldots,N \; countries. \qquad (4.1)$$

Technical capability depends on resources and the current state of technology, and it has two broad dimensions: domestic ($X_{i,d}$) and global ($X_{i,f}$) links, where d is for domestic, and f is for foreign links, so that $Y = F(X_d, X_f)$, ignoring the i-index. Domestic production in which global links are, respectively, absent and exogenously present would be (4.2a) and (4.2b) below:

$$Y = A\,F\left(X_d\right), X_f \subset A \tag{4.2a}$$

$$Y = X_f\,F\left(X_d\right), A \subset X_f, \tag{4.2b}$$

Economic performance and domestic resources ($X_{i,\,d}$)

Underlying domestic production relations are current and historical factors and forces of production. Current factors include land (*R*), economically active population (*N*), and physical capital (*K*). Historical factors include the initial conditions of production in each country, normally measured by the level of income in some reference (initial) year (Y_0). The assumption is that AY_0 depends on historical influences and legacies like colonial background (religion, language, political system, and such). Hence, we can now restate (4.2) as

$$Y = A\,F\left(R,N,K\right) \tag{4.3a}$$

$$Y = X_f F\left(R,N,K\right) \tag{4.3b}$$

Without loss of generality, I simplify (4.3) by noting that the supply of land as a primary factor of production is limited, so that it can be set equal to unity, and as in previous studies its effects on economic activity are constant and sufficiently picked up by other variables such as trade openness, landlockedness, and so on. If (4.3a), for example, is multiplicative in form, then it can be expressed as

$$Y = A\,K^{\alpha} N^{\beta}, \alpha + \beta \leq 1, \tag{4.4}$$

where *N* is assumed to consist of unskilled labor (*L*) and skilled labor defined as human capital (*H*), implying that $N = L^a H^b$. Hence, following Solow (1956, 1957) and others after him, I also assume that *L* evolves at an exogenous rate (*n*) equal to the rate of growth of *N*, that is,

$$L = e^{nt}\left(N\,H^{-b}\right)^{1/a}. \tag{4.5}$$

Hence, given (4.5), (4.4) becomes

$$Y = A\,K^{\alpha} e^{\beta_1 nt} N^{\beta_1/a} H^{(a\beta_2 - b\beta_1)/a}. \tag{4.6}$$

In per capita and natural logarithmic terms, (4.6) is

$$y = a + \alpha k + \beta_1 nt + \beta_2^* h, \frac{a\beta_2 - b\beta_1}{a} = \beta_2^* \tag{4.7}$$

where $y = \log(Y/N)$, $k = \log(K/N)$, $h = \log(H/N)$, a = productivity shifter, α = elasticity of capital, $\beta_1 t$ elasticity of raw labor, and $a\beta_2 - b\beta_1/a$ = elasticity of H, and $n = \beta_1$ = natural rate of growth of N over time $t \geq 1$.

Jones (1997), and Hall and Jones (1999) approximate H as the proportion of raw labor (L) that is skilled, where skills are gained through education, for example, so that

$$H = e^{\varphi S} L, \tag{4.8}$$

where S = educational attainment measured as the average number of years of schooling. However, (4.8) understates the level of H and overstates its statistical importance. Hence, the correct evolution of H is over the economically active population (N), i.e.,

$$H = e^{\varphi q} N. \tag{4.9}$$

This means that (4.9) is consistent with Romer (1989, 1990), Benhabib and Spiegel (1994), and Dinopoulos (1996) in its suggestion that H is quality N á lá Schultz (1981), Becker (1996), and others. The refining of N takes place through the usual processes and activities like education, training, experience, health, nutrition, and mortality-fertility. Hence, in (4.9) q is a vector of processes and activities that refine N, and n is the constant growth rate of L equal to the growth rate of N, according to the exogenous neoclassical growth model. Thus, going back to (4.6), plugging in H, simplifying, and normalizing (4.9) gives

$$y = a + \alpha k + \beta_2^{**} q + \beta_1 n, \beta_2^{**} = \frac{\varphi(a\beta_2 - b\beta_1)}{a}, t = 1. \tag{4.10}$$

In (4.6), (4.7), or (4.10), the state of technology (A, a) is the only domestic force. It is assumed to be nonstochastic and independent of L and H both contemporaneously and over time. Obviously, in developing countries (A, a) is likely associated with K, which itself is mainly imported. In addition, there are nontrivial relationships among A, H, and L, but I assume that (4.7) expresses the *i*th country's economic activity on the bases of primary domestic resources (factors and forces). The effects of these resources depend on the quality of surrounding institutions.

Economic Performance, Domestic Resources, and Governance (I)

There are many measures of governance, but only the World Bank's World Governance Indicators (WGI), and the Mo Ibrahim's governance index (MIGI) interest this essay. Clearly, different aspects of institution affect economic performance differently. Here I argue that the primary influence on production of institutions and institutional quality takes place through improving the quality of the population—I have likened that to mining population for human capital (Amavilah 2008a). In this way it is easy to see measures of governance as elements of q, so that (4.10) becomes

$$y = a + \alpha k + \theta_1 S + \theta_2 I + \beta_1 nt, t > 1, n \neq 0, \tag{4.11a}$$

$$y = a + \alpha k + \theta_1 S + \theta_2 I + \beta_1 n, t = 1, n \neq 0, \tag{4.11b}$$

where

$$\theta_1 = \left(\frac{\varphi_1 (a\beta_2 - b\beta_1)}{a} \right), \theta_2 = \left(\frac{\varphi_2 (a\beta_2 - b\beta_1)}{a} \right),$$

S and I are educational attainment and governance, respectively, and noting that in the case of $n = 1$, $\beta_1 t$ represents an exogenous trend of the Solow-Swan variety.

Economic Performance, Domestic Resources, Governance, and Global Links ($X_{i,f}$)

Equations (4.8) and (4.11) express the ith country's economic activity in terms of primary domestic resources (factors and forces) and surrounding institutions. To it I now add the fact that African countries no longer operate in isolation from the rest of the world. What are the impacts of global links on these countries, and how do they compare to those of domestic resources and institutions? To explore this question, I identify and introduce into (4.11) key aspects of international relations such that

$$y = a + \alpha k + \theta_1 S + \theta_2 I + \gamma x_f + \beta_1 nt, t > 1, n \neq 0, \tag{4.12a}$$

$$y = a + \alpha k + \theta_1 S + \theta_2 I + \gamma x_f + \beta_1 n, t = 1, n \neq 0, \tag{4.12b}$$

Contained in (X_f, x_f) I consider four global links. First, is a measure of the extent to which the ith country is integrated into the global economy. Such a measure is calculated by WDI as the difference between the rates of growth of exports and GDP. Second, is aid dependency, a percent of foreign aid in gross national income. Finally, I link the production of GDP to net international tourism, a percent of exports of tourism less imports of tourism. The task now turns to how to estimate (4.12).

ESTIMATIONS

Data on some variables of interest such as MIGI are available only for 2000, 2002, and 2007. In the name of consistency all estimations for this essay cover only these three years across 38 African countries.[4]

Data

The dependent variable (y) is per capita GDP, drawn from the PWT 6.2 (Heston, Summers, and Aten 2006). Key independent variables include per capita physical capital (k), represented by the percent of GDP that goes to fixed capital formation as listed in IMF's IFS (2007). Besides k there is H. However, the Mincerian approach measures of H as the improved labor force, with the process of improvement taking place mainly through education, but sometimes also via on-the-job training, health, and job seniority (Eq. 4.8). This approach underestimates the level of H and overstates its importance (see Amavilah 2008). Here I argue that H is the quality of the economically active population net of raw labor (N)—Eq. (4.9). It has two interactive components. The first component relates to the educational process and is normally proxied as years of schooling (S). But educational attainment is so much higher the better the quality of surrounding institutions. Hence, $H = f(S, I)$, where in some estimations $I \equiv$ MIGI and in others $I \equiv$ WGI.

WGI and MIGI have different dimensions listed in Table 4.1. Some dimensions are predictably (expected *a priori* to be) inversely signed; others are not as clear. This expectation is consistent with the "law of motion" by which H is built through education and depreciated by age (see Cohen 1996, 355). The only difference, and not a trivial one, is that technological progress slows the rate of H depreciation.

Since y is per capita GDP, and we really do not need data for either L or N, we can use the rate of population growth (n) with a coefficient β1t, or we can use a time dummy $\beta 1t$ variable (t) with a coefficient $\beta 1n$. Also, the data for the Xf, consisting of three other variables: net tourism, integration, and aid dependency, comes from WDI reports. In this case, as in all other appropriate cases, the data are real, rather than nominal.

Table 4.1 Governance Indicators

World governance indicators (WGI)
• Voice and accountability
• Political stability and absence of violence
• Government effectiveness
• Regulatory quality
• Rule of law
• Control of corruption
Mo Ibrahim's governance index (MIGI)
• Safety and security
• Rule of law, transparency, and corruption
• Participation and human rights
• Sustainable economic opportunity
• Human development

Source: Author's creation.

Specification and Method

Last, I assume the equations to be estimated are linear, at least in the parameters, so that the general specification is,

$$y = F\left(k, t, S, I, x_f\right) + \varepsilon \tag{4.13}$$

In addition, I assume normal error and apply the OLS estimator. In doing so, I further assume there is little autocorrelation, and no variable interactions. This is obviously a shortcoming, but one that is not addressed in this essay, although the usual *ad hoc* adjustments are made to address conventional econometric problems.

Procedure

The estimation proceeds in three interrelated steps. First, I consider the following three relations:

$$y = F\left(x_d\right) + everything\,else \tag{4.14a}$$

$$y = F\left(x_f\right) + everything\,else \tag{4.14b}$$

$$y = F\left(I\right) + everything\,esle \tag{4.14c}$$

Eq. (4.14) allows for the examination of each three broad sources of economic performance, *ceteris paribus*. Second, I estimate (14.4) as

$$y = F\left(x_d,\, x_f\right) + everything\,else, and \left(x_d x_f\right) = 0 \tag{4.15a}$$

$$y = F(x_f, I) + everything\ else,\ and (x_f I) = 0 \quad (4.15b)$$

$$y = F(x_d, I) + everything\ else,\ and (x_d I) = 0 \quad (4.15c)$$

By avoiding the interactions I sacrifice realism for simplicity. As a final step I turn to:

$$y = F(x_d, I, x_f) + everything\ else,\ and (x_d x_f I) = 0 \quad (4.16)$$

Eq. (4.16) is the title of this chapter.

RESULTS

Tables 4.2, Table 4.3, and Table 4.4 present estimated results. Tables 4.2 and 4.3 display *unsanitized* results. Although econometrically impure, my opinion is that unsanitized results are *the real results*; they have better policy relevance than sanitized results, reported in Table 4.4. While bleaching the results meets the requirement of good econometrics, it also kills, figuratively speaking, all the good germs needed for both effective policy and further research. In this case opportunity costs are truly ubiquitous.

Real (Unsanitized/Unbleached) Results

If one assumes that performance depends on domestic resources ($X_d x_d$) alone, it is clear that investment (k) and human capital (H) in its Education and Health components are key factors. These three variables explain up to 38 percent of the variations in y, with the impact of k being the largest and of Health the second largest.

Assume that y depends on the quality of institutions alone. Using a measure of average WGI governance reveals that a percentage improvement in the average quality of institutions contributes half a dollar to y, and explains 24 percent of variations in the relationship, leaving a large "measure of our ignorance," as Abramovitz (1986) would put it. Similarly, utilizing average MIGI a unit improvement in governance has an impact of 1.7 on y, with comparable explanatory power as the Buse-Rsquare shows. Thus, the impacts of average WGI and average MIGI are larger than those of X_d. If we disaggregate WGI governance into its six dimensions, the Buse R-square increases significantly to 62 percent. Measured corruption contributes positively to y. While troubling such a finding is not unusual.

Table 4.2 Africa's GDP: Resources, Institutions, and External Relations—2000, 2002, 2007. (Parentheses are T-ratios at 5% significance level, mean y = 7.3184)

Variable	*Model 1*	*Model 2*	*Model 3*	*Model 4*	*Model 5*	*Model 6*	*Model 7*
Constant	4.182 (6.4)	7.484 (68.9)	7.689 (122.8)	0.491 (0.4)	−0.794 (−0.8)	5.944 (29.4)	8.123 (86.5)
Investment	0.579 (7.628)						
Education	0.083 (2.552)						
Health	0.303 (1.882)						
WGI Average		0.559 (6.154)					
Corruption			0.011 (0.121)				
Regulatory			0.197 (1.951)				
Voice			−0.076 (−1.01)				
Stability			0.139 (2.760)				
Effectiveness			0.760 (6.107)				
Rule of Law			−0.256 (−1.78)				
MIGIAve				1.675 (5.715)			
Safety					−0.275 (−2.32)		
Rule of Law					0.559 (3.61)		
(Rights					0.013 (0.12)		
Opportunity					1.666 (10.11)		
Development					0.197 (0.783)		
Openness						0.293 (5.919)	
Integration							−0.024 (−2.85)
Aid-depend							−0.419 (−11.1)
Net Tourism							−0.003 (−1.42)
Buse R^2	0.3806	0.2494	0.6192	0.2227	0.6845	0.2351	0.5544
SEE	0.9799	0.9968	0.9536	0.9916	0.9748	0.9759	0.9821
DW[ρ]	1.197 [0.04]	1.121 [0.04]	1.132 [0.07]	1.112 [0.04]	1.198 [0.02]	1.228 [0.06]	1.276 [0.05]
Normal t	−4.513	−4.199	−3.656	−4.325	−3.991	−4.319	−4.296

Source: Author's creation.

Table 4.3 Africa's GDP: Resources, Institutions, and External Relations—2000, 2002, 2007. (Parentheses are T-ratios at 5% significance level, mean $y = 7.3184$)

Variable	*Model 1*	*Model 2*	*Model 3*	*Model 4*	*Model 5*	*Model 6*	*Model 7*	*Model 8*
Constant	7.833 (7.15)	8.375 (7.25)	−1.16 (−0.92)	−3.03(−2.4)	7.790 (14.2)	7.73 (12.33)	1.132 (1.14)	1.428 (1.65)
Investment	0.249 (1.92)	0.181 (1.44)	0.324 (3.92)	0.499 (6.34)	0.363 (4.13)	0.309 (3.79)	0.566 (5.56)	0.719 (9.76)
Education	0.207 (3.79)	0.318 (6.69)	0.108 (2.32)	−0.08 (−2.4)	0.198 (7.71)	0.258 (7.49)	0.141 (3.64)	0.024 (0.56)
Health	−0.42 (−1.6)	−0.64 (−2.4)	−0.03 (−0.18)	0.02 (0.09)	−0.20 (−1.7)	−0.19 (−1.3)	−0.17 (−0.1)	−0.26 (−1.4)
Openness	0.110 (1.69)	0.168 (2.93)	0.233 (4.44)	0.069 (1.07)				
WGIAverage	0.728(7.637)				0.490(7.179)			
Corruption		−0.01 (−0.1)				0.135 (1.9)		
Regulatory		0.557 (4.4)				0.443 (6.6)		
Voice		−0.32 (−3.6)				−0.38 (−5.9)		
Stability		0.131 (2.1)				0.149 (3.5)		
Effectiveness		0.838 (4.9)				0.540 (5.9)		
Rule of Law		−0.56 (−2.9)				−0.39 (−3.4)		
MIGIAverage			1.602(5.846)				1.449(7.841)	
Safety				−0.30 (−1.9)				−0.33 (−3.5)
Rule of Law				0.76 (4.7)				0.30(2.0)
Rights				0.030 (0.3)				0.23 (2.8)
Opportunity				2.04 (13.0)				1.14 (9.1)
Development				−0.18 (−1.1)				0.14 (1.5)
Integration						−0.03 (−3.8)	−0.02 (−2.8)	−0.03 (−5.8)
Aid-depend						−0.4 (−15.6)	−0.4 (−14.9)	−0.3 (−15.7)
Net Tourism					−0.01 (−4.9)	−0.01 (−4.8)	−0.01 (−3.9)	−0.01 (−2.3)
Buse R^2	0.5806	0.6223	0.4960	0.7323	0.9001	0.9027	0.8573	0.9372
SEE	1.0040	1.0040	0.9799	1.0085	0.9873	1.0179	0.9858	1.0334
DW[ρ]	1.029 [0.08]	1.195 [0.02]	1.045 [0.09]	1.223 [0.00]	1.381 [−0.0]	1.396 [−0.0]	1.349 [0.01]	1.341 [0.01]
Normal t	−4.328	−4.131	−4.137	−2.820	−3.3506	−2.624	−3.196	−3.144

Source: Author's creation.

Table 4.4 Africa's GDP: Resources, Institutions, and External Relations—2000, 2002, 2007. (Parentheses are T-ratios at 5% significance level, mean ln(GDP) = 7.3184)

Variable	*Model 1*	*Model 2*	*Model 3*	*Model 4*	*Model 5*	*Model 6*	*Model 7*
Constant	7.66 (136.82)	−0.548 (−0.87)	8.320 (7.42)	−2.891 (−2.98)	7.725 (12.34)	0.515 (0.75)	1.464 (1.80)
Investment			0.206 (1.71)	0.501 (6.19)	0.309 (3.79)	0.598 (6.47)	0.757 (10.55)
Education			−0.073 (−2.04)	−0.073 (−2.04)	0.258 (7.49)	0.129 (3.74)	
Health					−0.189 (−1.34)		−0.254 (−1.38)
WGIAverage							
Corruption					0.135 (1.89)		
Regulatory	0.131 (1.72)		0.511 (4.91)		0.443 (6.59)		
Voice			−0.345 (−4.14)		−0.384 (−5.91)		
Stability	0.211 (5.09)		0.149 (2.59)		0.149 (3.54)		
Effectiveness	0.897 (9.71)		0.936 (6.38)		0.540 (5.85)		
Rule of Law	−0.578 (−5.36)		−0.622 (−3.89)		−0.390 (−3.38)		
MIGIAverage						1.424 (8.06)	
Safety		−0.344 (−3.22)		−0.297 (−1.82)			−0.333 (−3.55)
Rule of Law		0.808 (7.25)		0.786 (5.69)			0.229 (1.60)
Rights							0.236 (2.98)
Opportunity		1.616 (13.61)		1.995 (12.08)			1.213 (11.53)
Development				−0.168 (−1.05)			0.125 (1.26)
Openness			0.149 (2.68)	0.066 (1.09)			
Integration					−0.033 (−3.79)	−0.024 (−3.38)	−0.035 (−6.08)
Aid-depend					−0.345 (−15.6)	−0.412 (−15.8)	−0.343 (−16.6)
Net Tourism					−0.01 (−4.84)	−0.009 (−4.58)	−0.006 (−2.47)
Buse R^2	0.6644	0.7284	0.6404	0.7045	0.9027	0.8630	0.9383
SEE	0.9914	0.9881	1.0071	0.99679	1.0179	0.9963	1.0239
DW[ρ]	1.248 [0.02]	1.201 [0.01]	1.244 [0.01]	1.223 [0.00]	1.396 [−0.04]	1.374 [−0.01]	1.338 [0.01]
Normal *t*	−3.755	−3.387	−3.744	−2.624	−2.624	−2.800	−3.876

Source: Author's creation.

Since it is statistically insignificant anyway, the usual interpretation applies. Moreover, the rule of law and freedom of expression constrain the growth of GDP. By the MIGI, the effects of human rights and economic development are positive, though statistically insignificant, while property rights are not safe and secure for the economic performance of these countries.

If one lets these countries interact with the outside world, and measure the extent of interaction with the PWT 6.2 indicator of openness, that measure is statistically significant to *y*. However, disaggregating openness and representing global links by the extent of integration, aid-dependency, and net tourism, openness becomes a major constraint on *y*. Specifically, this group of countries is not sufficiently integrated in the global economy to benefit from it. The countries are also too dependent on foreign aid, while net tourism is too narrow and too weak a driver of *y*. This makes sense since tourism is really trade in factor land in the classical sense, and as such subject to diminishing returns.[5]

Regressions in which *y* depends on investment, education, life expectancy, PWT 6.2 openness, and various WGI indicators of institutional quality, find the rule of law, freedom of expression, health, and corruption too constraining, the first three in a significant manner. MIGI measures of institutional quality produce similar results. Overall, for both MIGI and WGI, health, rule of law, and freedom of expression are the main obstacles to economic performance of this group of countries.

Bleached (Sanitized) Results

Table 4.4 documents some results sanitized for basic econometric problems by *ad hoc* adjustments like dropping variables whose effects are insignificant. Comparing these results to those in Tables 4.2 and 4.3 one notices considerable improvement in the statistical strength of the parameters. Across all models gross domestic investment in fixed capital has the largest positive effect. On average openness favors *y* generation in this group of countries. However, when disaggregated into the extent of integration of SSACs into the global economy, dependency on foreign aid, and net tourism, the results tell a different story, or different stories.

Also across countries WGI measures of institutional quality are very significant with government effectiveness being strongest followed by the rule of law, but of opposite signs. The explanatory power increases to 64 percent. This statistic is 70 percent for the MIGI variable, but in this instance it is education, safety and security, and human development level which are growth limiting.

CONCLUDING REMARKS

During the period under consideration, some African countries have performed well (Ruffing 2008). How are we to understand that performance? This chapter suggests that to understand what is happening one must see that economic performance depends on domestic resources, global links, and institutional quality. The results of the analysis reveal that gross investment has had the most consistent positive effect on the real incomes of these countries. This supports the conclusion reached by S. Devarajan, W. Easterly, and H. Pack (2002) that "low investment is not the constraint on African development." The education component of human capital is generally important, but only after the threshold of ten or more years of schooling. This may well be suggestive of Hanushek and Woessmann's (2008) study that shows that what matters for development is not quantitative, but qualitative, aspects of education (cognitive skills); test scores contribute more to the GDP growth than years of schooling and openness to trade (see their p. 639).

The results also shows that while openness in general is a good thing, openness to fierce competition through global integration and aid-dependency harms the performance of this group of countries. Almost all countries in the group have a surplus tourism export account, on average, however, the effects of net tourism on *y* are negative, which contradicts Fayissa, Nsiah, and Tadasse's (2007) study, although their sample size was larger than this one.

Improvements in the average quality of institutions, as measured by both the WGI and MIGI, have meant high *y*. At the disaggregate level, the results show that the rule of law and freedom of expression under the WGI institutional regime, and safety and security, and human development under the MIGI regime, have constrained *y*. I recognize two weaknesses of the results of this essay: Variable interactions were assumed away, and limited degrees of freedom were ignored. Notwithstanding these shortcomings, the implications for policy and further research are clear.

NOTES

1. The italicized phrases are due to Wayne A. Wickelgren's *How to Solve Mathematical Problems*, Dover Publications, Inc., 1995.

2. For detailed examples see UNU-WIDER's "Country Role Models for Development Success" series.

3. The phrase "fluid capital" is due to Lester D. Taylor of the University of Arizona, see his book cited here.

4. The thirty-eight countries included are: 1. Angola, 2. Benin, 3. Botswana, 4. Burkina Faso, 5. Burundi, 6. Cameroon, 7. Central African Republic, 8. Chad, 9.

Congo, Democratic Republic, 10. Congo, Republic of, 11. Cote D'Ivoire, 12. Eritrea, 13. Ethiopia, 14. Gabon, 15. Gambia, 16. Ghana, 17. Guinea, 18. Guinea Bissau, 19. Kenya, 20. Lesotho, 21. Madagascar, 22. Malawi, 23. Mauritius, 24. Mozambique, 25. Namibia, 26. Niger, 27. Nigeria, 28. Rwanda, 29. Senegal, 30. Sierra Leone, 31. South Africa, 32. Sudan, 33. Swaziland, 34. Tanzania, 35. Togo, 36. Uganda, 37. Zambia, and 38. Zimbabwe.

5. Note that most tourists go to these countries for nature trips, wildlife safaris, and ancient monuments—all forms of land, classically defined.

Chapter 5

Globalization, Governance, and Economic Performance

This chapter estimates and compares the effects of globalization, governance, and conventional factors and forces on the economic performance of SSACs. The analysis finds that both physical and human capital as well as unexplained technical residuals affect economic performance, although human capital and technical change do not always have statistically significant impacts. The policy implication of these results calls for improvement of all three variables. Economic performance also varies with measures of globalization, but it is social globalization rather than economic globalization that is most beneficial. On average, the quality of institutions are important to economic performance, but, when disaggregated, different measures of institutional quality have different effects on performance. Even as there remains a need to improve them, these results are reasonable.

The preceding chapter found domestic resources to be more important to economic performance than global links. A major argument against globalization is that it hurts poor people. Since most poor people live in developing countries, those against globalization portray their protestations as attempts to save poor countries. Meanwhile advocates of globalization charge that most developing countries are poor not because of globalization, but rather because of the poor quality of their institutions and the equally poor governance such institutions provide. For introductory yet incisive, debates about the links between globalization and poverty, I recommend Nissanke and Thorbecke (2008) and Ann Harrison (2007). Conspicuously, obvious from these readings and others is that stuck in the middle are policymakers for SSACs. Literally, here you have an appropriate circumstance for the African proverb which says that "when two bull elephants fight, it is the grass beneath them that suffers the most." Ironically, although the experiences of SSACs are often cited in support of both anti-globalization and governance arguments, comparative evidence of the effects of globalization and governance on the economic performance of SSACs remains scanty.

This chapter estimates and compares the effects of globalization and governance on the economic performance of thirty-five SSACs.[1] The analysis utilizes a production function approach in which the economic activity depends on measures of globalization, governance, and some conventional controls. It finds that globalization and governance significantly affect the performance of these countries, but different measures of globalization and governance have different impacts. The effects of physical capital are robust, while those of the health and education components of human capital tend to switch signs—but they are still economically relevant. Based on these findings, one can conclude that SSACs gain from increased globalization and improved governance, but conventional factors and forces are important as well.

The structure of the chapter is as follows: The first section briefly outlines the literature behind the empirical set-up in the next section. The fourth section presents the results and their implications for policy and further research. The last section draws a conclusion.

SOURCES OF THE RECENT ECONOMIC PERFORMANCE OF SSACS

I argue that the economic performance of SSACs during the period under study has depended on globalization, governance, and domestic resources serving as controls.

Economic performance and globalization

Although globalization means different things to different people (see, for example, Dreher, Gaston, and Martens 2008), there is now little doubt that it affects the economic performance of countries in important ways (Waters 1995). Dani Rodrik's (1997) "tensions of globalization" emanate not from the absence, but from the magnitude and distribution of the gains from globalization. Citing Zimbabwe as an example Arne Bigsten and Dick Durewall (2002) argue that poor policy against market integration, especially against "increased exposure to international prices and returns on assets" (p. 18) has led to the decline in economic performance in Zimbabwe. In this case weak economic performance, governance, and globalization are all three mutually reinforcing, creating a universe of negatives—the so-called Africa's growth tragedy (Easterly 1995).

Axel Dreher (2003) provides an excellent review of different angles of quantifying the effects of globalization on economic performance, and develops indices covering aggregate and disaggregate aspects of globalization for 123 countries during the 1970–2000 period. His analysis concludes that "globalization is good for growth [because] countries that globalized more, experienced high growth rates" (14). In this conclusion Rwanda and Zimbabwe were at the time among the least globalized, as well as among the weakest performing, countries. Dreher further observes that these two countries "have poor institutions which repress growth and promote poverty." The Swiss Economic Research Institute, or *Konjunkturforschungstell* (KOF), now publishes globalization data annually, and one key aspect of this essay is to estimate and compare the effects of Dreher-KOF globalization and governance as a measure of the effects of the institutional quality on the economic performance of thirty-five SSACs.[2]

Economic performance and governance

In his presidential address to the American Economic Association, Avinash Dixit (2009) observes that "good governance is needed to secure three essential prerequisites of market economies: Security of property rights, enforcement of contracts, and collective action" (5). Although Dixit also calls for a better understanding of how governance actually influences economic performance before anyone can recommend institutional reform, evidence points to institutions and institutional quality as essential elements of the growth of both output and resource productivity. This is not a new insight; classical economists like Adam Smith (1973 [1776]), and new classical economists like W. Arthur Lewis (1965 [1955]), as well as contemporary theorists like North (1990) and Gradstein and Konrad (2006) have touched upon the role in economic performance of institutions and institutional quality. Aron's (2000) empirical review of the links between institutions and the economic performance of developing countries demonstrates that countries with "good" institutions tend to do better than countries without or with "bad" institutions—that is, "institutions rule" (Rodrik, Subramanian, and Trebbi 2004; Glaeser, Lopez-Salines, and Shleifer 2004). What remains controversial is how to quantify the effects of institutions. For that some experts, like Sachs and Warner (1997) and Bloom and Sachs (1998), use geography to describe institutional effects on growth. Others like Nathan Nunn and Diego Puga (2012) quantify the "ruggedness" of geography to assess its relationship to the slave trade and hence economic performance, while still others turn to proxies like constitutions, political freedoms and social justice (North 1990; Persson and Tabillini 2003; Amavilah 2009; Siba 2008; Nava-Ruis 2007).

As described in the preceding chapter, governance has emerged from these discussions as the preferred measure of institutional quality—which justifies what is now called the Kaufman-Kraay-Zoido-Mastrzzi (KKZM) index of governance (see, for example, Kaufman and Kraay 2008). Quibria (2006, 104), for example, shows that a KKZM composite correlates positively with the economic growth of a number of Asian countries. As a popular version of KKZM, the World Bank's Worldwide Governance Indicators (WGI) is the most comprehensive of the eighteen or so common indices of governance. Over the years 1996–2006, the KKZM covered 212 countries and territories, and it has the following six dimensions: (a) voice and accountability, (b) political stability and absence of violence, (c) government effectiveness, (d) regulatory quality, (e) rule of law, and (f) control of corruption. All six dimensions, individually and collectively, can make a statement about economic performance. For instance, where the rule of law is absent or weak, property rights will be fragile, markets dysfunctional, and economic performance most likely unsustainable (Acemoglu, Johnson, and Robinson 2002). Moreover, Mo Ibrahim African Governance Index (MIGI) covers 48 SSACs, and addresses the biases that afflict competing indicators like the WGI.

Economic performance and domestic resource controls

The focus of this chapter is on the effects of globalization and governance on economic performance. However, in estimating the effects on economic performance of globalization and governance I use domestic resources as controls. The vast extant literature on the primary sources of economic performance suggests that pre-independence the growth of SSACs was extensive growth, coming from the growth of labor, land (mainly mineral and agricultural commodities), fixed capital in agriculture, and mining and quarrying (see Fafchamps 2000; Ndulu and O'Connell 1999; O'Connell and Ndulu 2000; Amavilah 1996). Tahari, Ghura, Akitoby, and Aka (2004) estimate that the slow growth of most SSACs that occurred during the years 1960–2002 depended on the accumulation of "objects" rather than "ideas"—to use Paul Romer's (1993) lingo. Only Botswana and Mauritius, and more recently Equatorial Guinea and the Gambia, grew at rates exceeding four per cent per annum over the same time period (Basu, Calamitsis, and Ghura 2000, Acemoglu, Johnson, and Robinson 2001a, b). Overall, physical capital accumulation contributed to growth more than labor.

Beginning c. 1997, the number of SSACs with growth rates above four per cent more than doubled. Again Tahari, Ghura, Akitoby, and Aka (ib.) associate that growth with improvements in institutional quality, human capital, and the macroeconomic policy environment, in addition to the broadening of the export base from a narrow range of raw commodities to semi-processed goods. A previous chapter presents evidence supporting the positive effects of macroeconomic policy on the performance of forty-six African countries in 2004/2005. Moreover, O'Connell and Ndulu (2000) and Ndulu and

O'Connell (1999) associate the performance of SSACs with capital accumulation, demographic changes, policy, institutions, political (in)stabiliy, and total factor productivity (TFP), where TFP is measured as the number of years of schooling. In that sense TFP is the same thing as human capital (*H*). In fact, Benhabib and Spiegel (1994) show that most African countries lack the critical mass of *H* stock required for fast-growing TFP.

EMPIRICAL FRAMEWORK

From both W. Arthur Lewis (1965) and Paul Romer (1990, 1993, 1994), it is clear that economic performance depends on factors and forces of production. A number of forces explain Africa's economic performance; key among them are technology and institutions, where technology is measured variously as TFP and or Solow residual (*A*), and institutions are often proxied by governance. In a recent paper, Jean-Claude Maswana (2006) associates the poor performance of African countries with lack of technological innovation and its underlying knowledge, and bad policies. These matters can all be reasonably accommodated in a production function model as the next subsection illustrates.

Model specifications

For a given state of technology (A_{it}), let the value of a production activity (Y_{it}) depend on a vector of domestic resources (X_{it}) serving as conventional controls, and on another vector of state variables (Z_{it}) such that over time (t)

$$Y_{it} = F\left(A_{it}X_{it}\right), Z_{it}), i = 1, 2, 3, \ldots, M; t = 1, 2, 3, \tag{5.1}$$

where i = 1, 2, 3, . . . , M are the number of SSACs, and t = 1, 2, 3 are time periods. From here designate $X_{it} = [N_{it}, H_{it}, K_{it}]$ and $Z_{it} = [Z_{1t}, Z_{2t}]$, for N_{it} = economically-active population, H_{it} = human capital, K_{it} = physical capital, Z_{1t} = measures of globalization, and Z_{2t} = measures of governance. Assuming (5.1) is multiplicative in form leads to

$$Y_{it} = \left(A_{it}N_{it}\right)^{\alpha} H_{it}^{\beta}K_{it}^{1-\alpha-\beta}. \tag{5.2}$$

Let's drop the country (i) and time (t) indices for neatness, and follow Amavilah (2008a) in stating H as a function of quality N, that is,

$$H = e^{\varphi q}N, \tag{5.3}$$

where q is a placeholder for the education (literacy rate or years of schooling) and the health (life expectancy at birth) dimensions of *H*. Now, if globalization and governance are significant to an economic activity, one likely transmission channel is A. Hence, one can argue that

$$A = e^{\gamma Z} = e^{\gamma_1 Z_1 + \gamma_2 Z_2}, \tag{5.4}$$

where for a Kaldorian economy the dynamics of *A* are according to the Verdoorn's Law of motion. Plugging (5.3) and (5.4) into (5.2) and simplifying gives

$$Y = e^{\alpha\gamma Z + \beta\varphi q} N^{\alpha+\beta} K^{1-\alpha-\beta} = e^{\alpha\gamma_1 Z_1 + \alpha\gamma_2 Z_2 + \beta\varphi q} N^{\alpha+\beta} K^{1-\alpha-\beta}. \tag{5.5}$$

The logarithmic *N* intensity of (5.5) is per capita gross domestic product (*y*)

$$y = \alpha\gamma Z + \beta\varphi q + (1-\alpha-\beta)k = \alpha\gamma_1 Z_1 + \alpha\gamma_2 Z_2 + \beta\varphi q + (1-\alpha-\beta)k, \tag{5.6}$$

where (5.6) is deterministic in that it has neither an intercept nor a random error term.[3] Then based on (5.6) the estimation equation is

$$y = \theta_0 + \theta_1 Z_1 + \theta_2 Z_2 + \theta_3 q + \theta_4 k + \mu \tag{5.7}$$

for θ_0 = constant, $\theta_1 = \alpha\gamma_1$ = effects of globalization, $\theta_2 = \alpha\gamma_2$ = effects of governance, $\theta_3 = \beta\varphi$ = effects on *y* of the education and health dimensions of *H*, $\theta_4 = (1 - \alpha - \beta)$ = the effect of physical capital investment on economic performance, and μ = the error term. I use the OLS estimator to estimate (5.7), making the usual adjustments for statistical problems. However, in this essay, I do not drop globalization and governance measures even when they are statistically insignificant.

Data and Data Sources[4]

The dependent variable (*y*) is real GDP per capita in terms of purchasing power parity (PPP), drawn from the Penn World Table (PWT) 6.2, where it appears as "rgdptt." Preliminary charts for the years under consideration here show that most SSACs fall in the US$2000 y range. There are fewer and fewer countries as one climbs the y ladder, of which Mauritius is the leader with a y of US$16400.

Variable (*K*, *k*) is a proxy for physical capital; it is measured as a percent of GDP that goes to domestic fixed investment. This data is available in the IMF's *International Financial Statistics Yearbook* (2007). Most SSACs spend an average of 19 percent on gross fixed capital formation, not uncommon among developing economies generally, but still at the lower end of K-formation compared to that of fast-growing developing economies.

Next, I consider two q dimensions of human capital (*H*): Education and Health. Health is measured as life expectancy at birth. Education is the average years of schooling. When data was missing the apparent average for Africa is used. Both the education and health statistics came from WDI reports. Again, preliminary sketches show that the average health of these countries is clustered between forty and sixty years, corresponding to a *y* of approximately US$2500. They also reveal that countries with under ten years of schooling have an average y of only $2200. Beyond ten years of schooling, y more than doubles, and or even triples for some SSACs.

Globalization (Z_1) data is Dreher-KOF data available and explained at KOF's website (http://globalization.kof.ethz.ch/) and in Axel Dreher (2003).[5] It comes in one aggregate and three disaggregates. The aggregate index is called the "Index of Globalization." The three disaggregates are the "Index of Economic Globalization," "Index of Social Globalization," and the "Index of Political Globalization."[6] Investigating plots of these variables reveal positive relationships between KOF globalization measures and *y*. In fact, there are only 3–4 SSACs with the level of globalization that corresponds to the $(log 6.5) to $(log 8.0) *y* range.

For governance (Z_2) I use the following two indicators of institutional quality: the WGI and the MIGI. As stated already, there are six dimensions for WGI. To these I have added a simple average WGI. This average WGI, like other dimensions, lies in the −2.5 to 2.5 interval. Further examination of these indices demonstrates that there is considerable variation across indices and countries. Even so, the average quality of institutions is positively related to y.

The MIGI on the other hand ranges from zero to 100 percent. Like WGI, MIGI also varies a lot across countries, and it is directly related to y. In spite of this positive correlation, most SSACs fall in the 0 to 2 and $665–$1808 governance-*y* range.

RESULTS

Estimation results are in tables 5.1, 5.2 and 5.3. Estimation 1.1, for example, shows that the health dimension of human capital has a positive, albeit statistically insignificant, effect on the economic performance of SSACs. However, the largest influence on performance comes from the average measures of globalization and WGI governance. Thus, y is highly elastic with respect to

Table 5.1 Resources, Globalization, and WGI Governance, and the Performance of SSACs—2000, 2002, 2007. (Parentheses are *t*-values at 5% significance level)

Variable	*Estimation 1.1*	*Estimation 1.2*	*Estimation 1.3*	*Estimation 1.4*
Constant	1.102(1.137)	0.755(0.645)	2.517(2.383)	1.915(1.554)
Controls				
• Capital	0.129 (1.850)	0.143(2.042)	0.266(2.969)	0.268(2.619)
• Education	0.052 (1.351)	0.177(4.046)	−0.018(−0.54)	0.097(2.093)
• Health	0.038 (0.196)	0.256(1.054)	0.444(2.384)	0.065(2.852)
Globalization				
• Average	1.528(11.342)	1.401(8.857)		
• Economic			0.013(0.076)	0.108(0.566)
• Social			1.302(8.928)	1.151(7.091)
• Political			−0.509(−4.66)	−0.537(−4.42)
Governance (WGI)				
• Average	0.433(6.677)		0.207(2.328)	
• Regulatory		0.104(0.999)		0.219(2.297)
• Voice		−0.302(−4.119)		−0.136(−1.65)
• Stability		−0.027(−0.55)		−0.039(−0.76)
• Effectiveness		0.675(5.246)		0.627(5.317)
Rule of Law		0.215(1.661)		−0.160(−1.26)
Summary Statistics				
• Buse R^2	0.6471[0.997]	0.7887[0.906]	0.7973[0.999]	0.7553[0.99]
• DW [ρ]	1.204[−0.012]	1.256[−0.029]	1.129[0.052]	1.344[−0.021]

Buse R^2 [] for the raw moments.
Source: Author's creation.

Table 5.2 Resources, Globalization, and MIGI Governance, and the Performance of SSACs—2000, 2002, 2007. (Parentheses are *t*-values at 5% significance level)

Variable	*Estimation 2.1*	*Estimation 2.2*	*Estimation 2.3*	*Estimation 2.4*
Constant	−4.577(−3.03)	−4.120(−3.99)	−1.071(−0.76)	−2.992(−2.49)
Controls				
• Capital	0.312(4.519)	0.274(4.428)	0.289(3.572}	0.385(4.519)
• Education	0.021(0.505)	−0.089(−2.85)	−0.014(−0.43)	−0.066(−1.84)
• Health	0.384(1.674)	0.291(1.779)	0.752(3.659)	0.383(1.735)
Globalization				
• Average	1.356(9.774)	1.172(7.450)		
• Economic			−0.071(−0.50)	−0.021(−0.13)
• Social			1.156(6.610)	0.452(2.502)
• Political			−0.655(−7.87)	−0.263(−2.66)
Governance (MIGI)				
• Average	1.077(3.519)		0.891(2.650)	
• Safety		−0.434(−3.69)		−0.286(−3.20)
• Rule of Law		0.875(4.717)		0.999(6.212)
• Rights		−0.165(−1.58)		−0.154(−1.66)
• Opportunities		1.312(9.563)		1.593(8.606)
• Development		−0.173(−0.99)		−0.163(−0.90)
Summary Statistics				
• Buse R^2	0.6333[0.999]	0.7317[0.998]	0.7515[0.999]	0.7939[0.99]
• DW [ρ]	1.047[0.063]	1.318[−0.036]	1.158[0.024]	1.389[−0.059]

Buse R^2 [] for the raw moments.
Source: Author creation.

Table 5.3 Resources, and Globalization or WGI Governance, and the Performance of SSACs—2000, 2002, 2007. (Parentheses are *t*-values at 5% significance level)

Variable	*Estimation 3.1*	*Estimation 3.2*	*Estimation 3.3*	*Estimation 3.4*
Constant	7.299(7.633)	7.317(6.493)	−2.892(−3.57)	1.728(1.728)
Controls				
• Capital	0.252(2.424)	0.131(1.115)	0.331(4.356)	0.282(2.804)
• Education	0.181(3.989)	0.251(6.037)	−0.006(−0.26)	−0.026(−0.74)
• Health	−0.161(−0.72)	−0.098(−0.35)	0.744(3.917)	0.456(2.206)
Globalization				
• Average			1.654(11.718)	
• Economic				−0.026(−0.17)
• Social				1.308(9.178)
• Political				−0.365(−4.04)
Governance (WGI)				
• Average	0.689(7.56)			
• Regulatory		0.339(3.105)		
• Voice		−0.239(−2.61)		
• Stability		−0.008(−0.14)		
• Effectiveness		0.717(4.74)		
• Rule of Law		0.021(0.0136)		
Summary Statistics				
• Buse R^2	0.5170[0.999]	0.6187[0.998]	0.6801[0.999]	0.5156[0.99]
• DW [ρ]	1.139[0.046]	1.177[0.029]	1.221[0.027]	1.264[−0.012]

Buse R^2 [] for raw moments.
Source: Author's creation.

globalization and governance. For instance, a unit improvement in globalization and governance increases y by two-fifth of one percent.

At the disaggregate level the positive effect of average WGI breaks down into the positive effects of the rule of law, government effectiveness, and the quality of the regulatory regime, as well as the negative effects of stability and freedom of expression. Ignoring the constant term, human and physical capital are important to economic performance. Moreover, when I disaggregate globalization and WGI governance (Estimation 1.3), it becomes clear that political globalization, voice, stability, and the rule of law undermine the economic performance of SSACs. This is the problem addressed in Amavilah, Asongu, and Andres (2017) for a larger sample which concludes that globalization aids economic peace and stability.

Across table 5.1 the effects of capital investment on economic performance range from 13 percent to 27 percent—a range that includes the 19 percent average for SSACs. Aggregate *H* also has a positive net effect on performance, but as Estimation 1.3 shows, the effects of the education component of *H* are negative whenever one disaggregates globalization and the WGI governance, which are both very strong. Globalization appears to substitute education. Social globalization has the strongest effect, and political globalization has a negative effect. The regulatory quality of institutions, freedom of expression, political stability and peace, and the rule of law also have adverse impacts on the performance of this group of SSACs.

In table 5.2 economic performance depends on conventional factors and forces, globalization, and MIGI measures of institutional quality. However, among conventional factors the impact of education on performance continues to be negative when *H* is disaggregated. Even so, the net effect of *H* on performance is positive, while that of capital investment at 28–39 percent is higher than it is in table 5.1. Moreover, average and social globalization, and average MIGI governance maintain their dominance, while political globalization, rule of law, participatory and human rights, as well as the level of economic development, are drags on economic performance. Quite obviously, WGI and MIGI are neither substitutes nor comparable, but they yield consistent estimates. These estimates suggest that globalization and governance are important to the economic performance of these countries but their effects differ according to the types of globalization and governance.

From table 5.3 the effects of the health and education components of *H* keep switching signs depending on the inclusion of globalization and governance. However, since when negative the effects of disaggregated *H* are also statistically insignificant, the economic meaning of the results is unaltered, and it suggests that *H* is a major growth concern for SSACs. However, the explanatory power of the regressions falls, in some cases dramatically, so that the constant term is nearly the same size as the mean of the dependent variable. The usual *ad hoc* adjustments reported in Table 5.4 do not improve the results, although in this case the constant term is biased downward. This all leaves us with substantial confidence in the overall exercise even as we admit the need for improved statistical significance of individual parameters.

CONCLUDING REMARKS

Utilizing a production function approach in which economic activity depends on measures of globalization, governance, and some conventional controls, this essay estimates and compares the effects of globalization and governance on the economic performance of thirty-five SSACs. Regarding controls the analysis finds that both physical and human capital, as well as unexplained (exogenous) technical residuals, affect economic performance, although human capital and technical change do not always have statistically significant impacts. The policy implication of these results calls for improvement in all three variables.

Economic performance also varies substantially with measures of globalization. For instance, the average measure of globalization has a very strong effect on economic performance—good news for the proponents of globalization. However, disaggregating average globalization reveals that economic globalization and social globalization have positive effects on economic performance, while political globalization has a negative effect. Globalization is good for economic performance, but it is social globalization that is important for this group of countries in this time period. These results make good sense; political globalization and economic globalization have been going on across the world via international trade, finance, and diplomacy for many years. Social globalization is a recent phenomenon, intensified by the emergence and diffusion of new technologies and social networks. Hence, its marginal returns are high, and increasing in some cases.

The quality of institutions is also important to economic performance. Both average WGI and average MIGI have positive impacts. However, disaggregated, different measures of institutional quality have different effects on performance. The effects of WGI governance as regulatory quality and government effectiveness are always positive, while freedom of expression and political stability are negative. According to MIGI governance, safety and security of property rights, human rights, and the low level of economic development are the drags on the economic performance of SSACs. Overall, the results make sense and are credible, although there remains a need for fine-tuning the model, increasing the number of countries in the sample, and lengthening the time-series, and deploying alternative models and estimation techniques, which must be a separate pursuit altogether.

NOTES

1. The thirty-five countries are: 1. Benin, 2. Botswana, 3. Burkina Faso, 4. Burundi, 5. Cameroon, 6. Central African Republic, 7. Chad, 8. Congo, Democratic Republic, 9. Congo, Republic of, 10. Cote D'Ivoire, 11. Ethiopia, 12. Gabon, 13. Gambia, 14. Ghana, 15. Guinea Bissau, 16. Kenya, 17. Lesotho, 18. Madagascar, 19. Malawi, 20. Mauritius, 21. Mozambique, 22. Namibia, 23. Niger, 24. Nigeria, 25. Rwanda, 26. Senegal, 27. Sierra Leone, 28. South Africa, 29. Sudan, 30. Swaziland, 31. Tanzania, 32. Togo, 33. Uganda, 34. Zambia, and 35. Zimbabwe.

2. See KOF Index of Globalization at http://globalization.kof.ethz.ch/.

3. Equations (5.3)–(5.6) are simplifications. My thoughts are influenced by Michel Kalecki (1971) in that H(N), K(L), and A(q, and interaction among qs).

4. Exploratory charts are available in a working paper version of this essay online at http://econpapers.repec.org/paper/pramprapa/15600.htm and a spreadsheet is also available from the author upon request

5. I acknowledge greatfully Dr. Axel Dreher for helping me understand KOF data via email messages, and the collegial friendship developed that from those brief e-conversations.

6. In previous studies, I included regional dummies in (6), but the results were not informative enough to warrant doing so here.

Chapter 6

Spread of Innovations and Economic Performance

This chapter does two things. First, it argues that innovations spread more like wild fire than like systematic epidemics with some environments more susceptible to catching fire than others. Just as the rate of the spread of fire is a function of fuel and other factors, so too is the spread of innovations, only that in the latter case the fuel is human population. Human population in general is a necessary fodder for the spread of innovations. The sufficient condition is the quality of the population which can favor or disfavor the spread of innovations. Second, the rate at which innovations spread is subject to the forces of exhibition and inhibition. Exhibitors promote the spread of innovations; inhibitors subjugate them. Hence, where the forces of subjugation are stronger than the forces of promotion, it is the slow spread, rather than the lack, of innovations which undermines the competitiveness of nations, and consequently frustrates economic performance. This suggests a need for a simple and more realistic model.

This chapter and the next are invitational; it attempts to inspire both policy and future research that would sustain good economic performance. The maintained assumption is that it appears SSACs have finally found the growth recipe that has evaded them for decades. This sixth chapter is about the prospects and challenges for adopting and spreading the recipe. A key innovation is a gentle warning to SSACs that the spread of innovations and technologies will be uneven and like wildfires largely unpredictable. Success is attainable, because African countries are not different from other countries! The technologies and other innovations they need to grow already exist; there is no need to reinvent the wheel as the cost of reinventing the wheel, even with significant imitation, is higher than the cost of transferring innovations. A key obstacle to growth has been the constrained spread of innovations. This chapter does two things. First, it demonstrates theoretically the incompleteness of existing models of the spreads of innovations. Second, it illustrates the factors that tend to inhibit (exhibit) the spread of innovations.

Conventional theory almost always suggests that the spread of innovation follows a logistic (S-shaped) distribution. In the beginning there are few adopters; innovations pick up speed as the number of adopters increase; and finally the diffusion rate falls subject to capacity constraints. This theory draws mainly from traditional population growth models interspersed with epidemiological insights. However, not all is hunky dory with these models. Gupta, Sharma, and Karisiddappa (1997), for example, examine six conventional diffusion models using publications data on science and technology. While all six models describe an S-curve phenomenon, the authors "observed that [except for the modified exponential-logistic model] the models were not able to capture the fluctuations in the growth data" (526). Recently H. Peyton Young (2004, 2005, 2007) has injected life in the modeling process by introducing a novel dimension: Social learning. In this case, diffusion rates depend not only on the conventional rates of change of the Velhurst-Pearl-Reed variety, but also on heterogeneous thresholds associated with payoff matrices that give incentives for, disincentives against, or even discontinuation of, innovations (cf., Rogers 1983, 2003). This approach clearly advances understanding of the spread of innovations and helps explain the differential spread of innovations across populations (nations) or segments within one population.

Another troubling aspect of the logistic model of the spread of innovations, with or without social learning, is that the structural order of the model preordains its outcome. This is rather too artificial a result, because almost all models of innovations identify four elements of how [and why] innovations spread: the innovation itself, the channels through which the innovation is communicated, the time over which the innovation is communicated, and the social system that surrounds it all (Rogers 1983, 2003). Although less quantifiable than the first three elements, the social system is capable of constraining or promoting both the innovation and the channels of communication, and the economic time (run) over which all that happens. How quickly and successfully adoption occurs and whether a particular innovation takes-off or not, bears directly on the social system, and the dynamic nature of the social system suggests that innovations spread more like wild fire than like systematic contagions, with or without "heterogeneous thresholds"—Young's phrase.

The objective of this essay is to model that hypothesis by incorporating into the logistic model the wild fire analogy. The first section describes the conventional logistic model, and its Young extension. The first subsection of the third section shows the applicability of a basic fire spread model to innovation spread models. The second subsection of the same modifies the logistic model in a manner consistent with the fire spread model. It turns out that the fire spread component of the model is just a human capital dimension in the innovation spread model. The fourth section describes the (least squares) estimation of the modified logistic model, while the fifth section outlines the distributions that are consistent with the logistic model. Without denying either the relevance of conventional logistic models or the importance of social learning, this chapter shows that social learning makes the spread of innovations less predictable. Again, the reason is that innovations spread more like wild fire than like systematic contagions, with or without "heterogeneous thresholds." The last part of the chapter focuses on the factors that tend to inhibit (exhibit) the spread of innovations and makes a concluding remark.

INCOMPLETE MODELS OF INNOVATIONS

What is the rate of spread of an innovation X, such as a new technology, idea, or product? How and why do diffusion rates vary across populations and even within one population? Conventional theory suggests that the spread of innovations follows a logistic model with time as one, if not the key, determinant. According to this model an innovation appears from some exogenous source. A few members of a population adopt the innovation. First the innovation catches on slowly, then faster and faster as more and more people convert to it. In time, diminishing returns of a sort set in and the diffusion rate slows as it approaches its asymptote, leaving behind an S-shaped trace.

To demonstrate the preceding paragraph formally, assume we have a population with a maximum absorptive capacity of K(Z) at any time. Let all these people be potential adopters of an innovation (X).[1] Most likely out of K(Z), N(Z) people are actual adopters of an innovation X at any time. These N(Z) people spread X across at least some K(Z). Assume that each Nth spreader spreads X to λ(Z) individuals, and some of λ(Z) become spreaders themselves. Over time, the total number of spreaders (A(Z)) is

$$A(Z)=\lambda(Z)N(Z), \tag{6.1}$$

where Z is a multidimensional matrix of variables, including time, t, that determine the spread of an innovation. Given (6.1) the proportion of K(Z) that is not N(Z) is $[K(Z)-N(Z)]/K(Z)$. The number of new adopters ($A^*(Z)$ is

$$A^*(Z)\equiv\frac{dN}{dZ}=\lambda N(K_N)=\theta NK-\theta N^2,\theta=\frac{\lambda}{K}. \tag{6.2}$$

From (6.2) $dA^* / dN = \Theta K - 2\Theta N = 0 \Rightarrow K/2$. Since $dN / dZ = \Theta NK - \Theta N^2$, $dN = [\Theta NK - \Theta N^2]dZ$ such that

$$N(Z) = \int A^*(Z)dZ = \frac{K}{\alpha + \beta e^{-\gamma Z}} = \frac{1}{\left(1 + \beta e^{-\gamma Z}\right)} \quad (6.3)$$

for K = 1, $\alpha = 1$ and $\beta = -1 + 1/N(Z=0)$. Thus, (6.3) is a simple contagion version of the conventional Velhurst-Pearl-Reed logistic model (see Young 2004, 2005, 2007). It assumes that all λ(Z) individuals who learned about X from N(Z) convert at an instantaneous rate of γ. The Bass model generalizes (6.3) by assuming that conversion rates differ depending upon whether learning is from a familiar (internal) source or it is from an unfamiliar (external) source. Following Young let $\gamma_1 > 0$ be the conversion rate when learning is internal and $\gamma_2 > 0$ when learning is from an external source. Then (6.3) can be restated as

$$\frac{1}{1 + \varphi\gamma_2 e^{-(\gamma_1 + \gamma_2)Z}}, \gamma_i > 0, \varphi > 0. \quad (6.4)$$

Young then shows that for N(Z=0), $\varphi = 1/\gamma_2$ and (6.4) turns into

$$N(Z) = \frac{1 - e^{-\gamma^* Z}}{\pi e^{-\gamma^* Z}}, \gamma^* = \gamma_1 + \gamma_2, \pi = (\gamma_2 + \gamma_1\gamma_2)/\gamma_2 \quad (6.5)$$

Eq. (6.5) = (6.4) = (6.3) if $\gamma_2 = 0$, $\gamma_1 = \gamma > 0$, K = 1, and $\alpha = 1$. When $\gamma_1 = \gamma = 0$, and $\gamma_1 = \gamma_2 > 0$, $N(Z) = 1 - \exp(-\gamma Z)$, suggesting that everyone who could learn had learned, but the adoption rate has slowed down a lot, or it is taking place with a significant time lag. At this point Young introduces "social learning with heterogenous thresholds," so that the rate of the spread of an innovation is subject to some constraints like resistance, friction, and uncertainty. The introduction of thresholds specifically challenges the fundamental assumption of the simple contagion model "that people adopt an innovation simply because they heard about its existence" (9). Barriers to diffusion are lower the higher the penalty for not converting, or similarly the higher the payoff for converting. Thus, the rate of spread is either reduced or accelerated by "heterogeneous thresholds," which is Young's Equation (14, p. 13), and can be restated as

$$N(Z) = \frac{vF(N(Z)) - N(Z+1)}{v+1}. \quad (6.6)$$

Equation (6.6) approximates the number of individuals, given today's payoff, that can be expected to overcome their resistance and convert tomorrow. This is my simplification of Young, of course.

INNOVATIONS SPREAD LIKE WILD FIRE

This section has two parts. The first part next below shows the applicability of a basic fire spread model to innovation spread models, and the second modifies the logistic model in a manner consistent with the fire spread model.

Fire versus Innovations—An Analogy

Young's formulation shows that N(Z) depends on both the conventional rate γ and some resistance (assisting) factor. The formulation is understandable because innovations are human creations, and as such they depend on human population whose numbers and behavior are difficult to predict. While an innovation may be governed by logistic rules in some stages of its spread, other stages may be dynamic, perhaps even chaotic and ungovernable. A close view of Young's and Gupta, Sharma, and Kirisiddappa's graphical fits of diffusion models shows that the models miss the data in the middle of the S-curve. Therefore, it is not unreasonable to claim that innovations spread like wild fire. In fact, incorporating the wild fire phenomenon into the logistic models is like incorporating uncertainty, instead of risk, in Young's model. As Robert Frank (2007) explains in *Black Swans*, uncertain matrices almost always have relevant, albeit unknown and unpredictable, information content. They are like wildfires.

In its basic form, a fire spread model relates physical and behavioral properties of the fire to its environment, pre-ignition and during the burning process. Although there are many and increasingly sophisticated models of fire spread, almost all of them are based on Rothermel (1972). The Rothermel model states the fire spread (R) as the energy intensity of the reaction of fire (Ω), adjusted for factors that favor or hinder the spread of fire such as wind and slope (ψ), to fuel (U), that is,

$$R = \Omega(1 + \Psi)U^{-1}. \tag{6.7}$$

Essentially, (6.7) is a fire-over-fuel model. The question then becomes: How do we make these fire properties consistent with economic properties of the spread of an innovation? The answer turns out surprisingly simple. With respect to innovations, R is equivalent to the reaction intensity of a population to an innovation as described by Rogers (1983, 2003). Since a population's reaction to an innovation depends on the expected benefit/cost ratio, R acts like a measure of productivity. It is the expected intensity of use (X/N), where X is a measure of the innovation output. As such it reflects socioeconomic factors that facilitate or hinder the adoption and spread of X: culture, politics, religion, and so on (Bulliet 2002). Just like in the fire case, the spread of an innovation over a population (fuel) is an energy conservation problem.

MODIFIED LOGISTIC MODEL OF THE SPREAD OF INNOVATIONS

Taking (6.7) into account we can adjust (6.5) such that

$$N^*(Z) = RN(Z) = \frac{\Omega(1+\Psi)}{U}\frac{K}{\alpha+\beta e^{-\gamma Z}}. \tag{6.8}$$

Hence, $N^*(Z) \Leftrightarrow N(Z)\ \forall R= 1$. But in the standard model such as (6.3), K/α is the upper limit and $K/(\alpha+\beta) = N(Z=0)$. According to (6.8) the upper limit is $RK/(\alpha+\beta) = N(Z=0)$, and $RK/(\alpha+\beta) < K/\alpha$ for $0 < R < 1$. This clearly means that R simply refines N(Z) for quality, and is consistent with T.W. Schultz's (1981) concept of "quality population" or human capital (cf. Becker 1993) .

Now, from Jones (1997), among many, human capital (H(Z)) is

$$R \equiv H(Z) = e^{\eta q}L(Z), \tag{6.9}$$

where η is the human capitalization rate (appreciation/depreciation rate), and q include factors such as years of schooling, literacy rate, or health indicators like life expectancy, and fertility/mortality rates. However, although a reasonable proxy for human capital in production, L(Z) is too narrow a basis for H(Z) in characterizing the spread of an innovation. Children can spread innovations to other children and to their own parents. In this case both the past and the present depend on the future instead of the usual case in which the past determines the future; advertisers and marketing people understand this fact too well. Those involved in the production of a new technology may not necessarily be its first adopters. Many scientists and engineers who built the first atomic bomb had in fact opposed its adoption long before and after it was used against Japan in WWII. Thus, a broader basis of H(Z) is needed and we call that "quality population" (G(Z)) so that

$$H(Z) = e^{\eta q}G(Z), \tag{6.10}$$

Hence, in terms of (6.3) or (6.4), (6.10) is really,

$$N^{**}(Z) = \frac{e^{\eta q}G(Z)K}{\alpha = \beta e^{-\gamma Z}} = \frac{H(Z)K}{\alpha + \beta e^{-\gamma Z}} = \frac{K^*}{\left(\alpha + \beta e^{-\gamma Z}\right)}, K^* = H(Z)K. \quad (6.11)$$

ESTIMATING AN H-MODIFIED LOGISTIC MODEL OF THE SPREAD OF INNOVATION

Given (6.11)

$$\frac{dN^{**}(Z)}{dZ} = \left(-\frac{K^*}{\left(\alpha + \beta e^{-\gamma Z}\right)^2}\right)\left(-\gamma\beta e^{-\gamma Z}\right) \quad (6.12)$$

Simplification of (6.12) shows that $(-K^* / \left(\alpha + \beta e^{-\gamma Z}\right)^2 = -\left(N^{**}(Z)\right)^2 / K^*$. Then from (6.12)

$$K^* = \alpha N^{**}(Z) + \beta N^{**}(Z)e^{-\gamma Z} \Rightarrow \beta e^{-\gamma Z} = \frac{K^*}{N^{**}(Z)} - \alpha. \quad (6.13)$$

Plugging $-(N^{**}(Z))^2 / K^*$ and $-\gamma(K^* / N^{**}(Z) - \alpha)$ into (6.13) and simplifying leads to

$$\frac{dN^{**}(Z)}{dZ} = \frac{\left[\left(\gamma N^{**}(Z)\right)K^* - \alpha\gamma\left(N^{**}(Z)\right)^2\right]}{K^*}. \quad (6.14)$$

Given K^* in (6.13),

$\alpha = \dfrac{K^* - \beta N^{**}(Z)e^{-\gamma Z}}{N^{**}(Z)}$ and $\beta = \dfrac{K^* - \alpha N^{**}(Z)}{N^{**}(Z)e^{-\gamma Z}}$. But $K^* \equiv H(Z)K$, implying that

$$K^* = \frac{\left[N^{**}(Z)\left(\alpha + \beta e^{-\gamma Z}\right)\right]}{e^{\eta q}G(Z)} \quad (6.15)$$

Consequently,

$$N^{**}(Z) = \left(\frac{N^{**}(Z)\left(\alpha - \beta e^{-\gamma Z}\right)}{\alpha + \beta e^{-\gamma Z}}\right) \approx (6.12). \quad (6.16)$$

As one useful digression, we can also set H(Z) = α ≡ I, for "I" called "initial conditions" (Masterton-Gibbons 1995). Then it becomes clear that

$$N^{**}(Z) = \frac{IK}{\left[I + (K - I)e^{-\gamma Z}\right]}, K - I = \beta,$$

which is just a restatement of (6.12) or (6.16). Either (6.12) or (6.16) is a Markov property of the spread of innovation. It says that the spread of innovations depend only on the current activity, and not on history—a "memoryless" process, to use Masterton-Gibbons term.

The Distribution of the H-modified Logistic Model of the Spread of Innovation

Our discussion so far has assumed a logistic distribution without being specific. This is not maintainable because while N(Z) may follow a logistic distribution, H(Z) may follow a different distribution such that the product of the two, (H(Z)N(Z)) = n(z), may follow yet another distribution. Assume n(z) is lognormally distributed and let

$$a_0 = 1/(\sigma\sqrt{2\pi}\exp\left(\frac{\mu^2}{2\sigma^2}\right), a_1 = \frac{1}{2\sigma^2}, and\, a_2 = \frac{\mu}{\sigma^2}.$$

Then

$$n(z) = K^* / \left[a_0 exp\left(a_1 (lnz)^2 + a_2 lnz\right)\right], \tag{6.17}$$

If K^* = KH is also lognormal, then (6.17) becomes

$$n(z) = exp\left(a_1 (lnz)^2 + a_2 lnz + \eta q)\right],$$

which in logarithmic terms is

$$\ln n(z) = lna_0 + a_1 (lnz)^2 + a_2 lnz + \eta q. \tag{6.18}$$

One reason why Young (ib.) stresses a free-distribution of the F(.) of his model is that a logistic spread of innovation is similar to the Gompertz (Harris 1992; Thompson 1998). A Gompertz is a model of form

$$n^*(z) = e^{\alpha - \beta\gamma^Z}. \tag{6.19}$$

Consequently, the derivative of (6.19) is

$$\frac{dn^*(z)}{dlnz} = -\beta \ln \gamma\gamma^z e^{\alpha-\beta\gamma^z} = -\beta ln\gamma\gamma^z n^*(z). \tag{6.20}$$

The logistic and Gompertz models belong to the family of modified exponential model (Harris 1992; Young 2004, 2005, 2007). For example, if Y is any raw data, then the data transformation in (6.21) below shows the relationship between the Gompertz and logistic models, and the association of both to the modified exponential model (Harris 1992; Barnerjee 200x; Koch and Lind 1971; Gupta, Sharma, and Kirisiddappa 1997), that is,

$$n^{**}(z) = \frac{K^*}{Y} = \frac{K^*}{\alpha - \beta\gamma^Z}; lnY = lnn^*(z) = \alpha - \beta\gamma^Z. \tag{6.21}$$

From (6.21) and for H(Z)K = K*, the logistic form of the Gompertz is

$$n^{**}(z) = \frac{e^{\eta q} G(z) K}{lne^{\alpha-\beta\gamma^z}}. \tag{6.22}$$

Since $lnn^{**}(z) = G(Z) - lnK + \eta q - \ln(\alpha - \beta\gamma^z)$, one can show that

$$n^{**}(z) = -\ln(\alpha - \beta\gamma^z) = \frac{1}{\alpha - \beta\gamma^z}. \tag{6.23}$$

FUNCTIONAL FORM OF H(Z) AND INHIBITED (EXHIBITED) SPREAD OF INNOVATIONS

The discussion so far assumes that H(Z) is linear in G(Z) so that η is a constant. There is no reason not to think that H(Z) can be raised to some power. Unfortunately pursuing this question does not add any more to clarity than leaving it unattended. Instead, one might stress that the roots of economic progress, as G. L. Bach (1960) once put it, are resources, technology, specialization, and exchange. However, the recent literature is abundantly clear that the competitiveness of nations is mainly a matter of technology and technological capability (Charrtrand 2002, 2006). The problem then is not so much that technology is scarce; nor is it the lack of technological innovations. The last two centuries alone have produced unprecedented technological innovations in superfluous quantities and qualities (Moykr 2005). The real difficulty is the uneven diffusion of innovations. For this reason "some countries prosper while others fall behind" (Fagerberg, Srholec, and Knell 2007). Unfortunately, current models of the spread of innovations lack generalizable properties that would admit to the fact that not only do innovations, like wildfires, spread in unpredictable ways, the spread itself is often subject to systematic and systemic inhibitors and exhibitors for which simpler and more realistic models than those readily in use are needed. While not promising to present a novel model of diffusion of innovations, this discussion contributes to the outline of how one may proceed to synthesize existing models to address the problem.

The modification is possible because the diffusion of innovations among human beings is not a fundamentally different process from what it is among other social beings like honey bees, for instance. It is a discrete and disjointed process that is not amenable to easy modeling despite what continuous-time mathematics suggests. First, one must have a well-functioning colony (community) of individuals with pressing needs and desires (Scarcity is good!), and the willingness and ability to meet those needs and desires. When supported by the ability and willingness to satisfy them, needs compel different types of learning behavior as a matter of self-preservation. Learning leads to the discovery of innovations, which in turn enables adoption, and then diffusion.[2] The process is multi-phased, and each phase in the process requires learning. Learning occurs at different levels, and progresses at different rates.

Let's take a simple example from honey bees. Assume a bee colony of N_0 well-functioning members. The bees have to live (survive), and so they have to know how to learn first and foremost. The bees specialize to lower the cost of living, improve efficiency, the whole shebang. This means they have an effective "rule of law" and institutional mechanisms for monitoring and enforcing laws. To produce honey some n_0 field bees go out looking for flowers, a task they must be capable of performing. When field bees depart, they leave behind $N_1 = N_0 – n_0$ community members to do other things. Meanwhile dN_0 of N_0 and dn_0 of n_0 bees will die.[3] The death of dN_0 reduces the population to $N_1(1–d)$, leaving fewer mouths to feed, but also fewer bodies to store collected juices and to convert the juices into honey. The death of dn_0 leaves $n_0(1–d)$ field bees, which constrains the learning process and hence diffusion by depreciating knowledge to find or report the whereabouts of flowers.

And that is not the end of the constraints, because when $n_1 = n_0(1–d)$ returns from the scouting mission to deliver news of the whereabouts of followers, now there are $N_2 = (N_0–n_0)(1–d) < N_1(1–d) < N_0$ members. The next mission party will consist of surviving scouts (n_1), and pollen collectors and juice makers (n_3), that is, $n_2 = n_1 + n_3 = n_0\left(1-d\right) + n_3$. However, for diffusion purposes only $n_4 = n_2\left(1-d\right) = \left(n_1 + n_3\right)\left(1-d\right)$ bees will return home to their colony of $N_3 = \left(N_0 - 2n_0\right)\left(1-d\right) - n_3$ members.[4] The logical moral of the story is that there are forces that inhibit and or exhibit learning, adoption, and hence the diffusion of innovations. Some inhibitions and exhibitions are systematic such as death; others are systemic such the organizational structure of a particular society which defines specialization, sets, and enforces the rules of the game (cf. Taylor and Levitt 2004). In the end, the potential future sources and sinks of innovations, and subsequently their limits are generally $N_i(t+1)\Delta N_i(t)\omega - n_i(t)$.

Learning and Adopting from Internally Homogeneous Sources

The diffusion of innovations among humans faces similar challenges and opportunities. How generalizable the bee example is to the human experience is the problem this essay discusses. Let's take a look. $N(t)$ are members of a given economic community like a country at time t. Let $n(t) \in N(t)$ be the number of economic agents who have heard (learned) of an innovation at that time, for $t_1 < t_2, n(t_1) < n(t_2)$. Ignoring writing variable t for convenience, unless where necessary, the number of adopters dn is such that $dn/n = \Delta N/n, \Delta N = N - n$. Then

$$dn = \alpha n \Delta N dt, \alpha > 0. \tag{6.24}$$

Therefore, the rate of change in the number of adopters becomes

$$\frac{dn}{dt} = \alpha n \Delta N. \tag{6.24'}$$

The solution to the differential (6.24) is

$$n = \frac{Ne^{\alpha Nt}}{(N-1)e^{\alpha Nt}}, \tag{6.25}$$

which represents the cumulative number of adopters. Thus, (6.25) assumes learning from internally homogeneous sources. It is the standard model of the diffusion of technological innovations used to describe the adoption of weed spray in Iowa and hybrid corn in Iowa, Kentucky, and Alabama in the 1950s, for instance (Rogers 1983, 2003; Burghes and Borrie 1981).

Learning and Adopting from Heterogeneous Sources

If learning is from heterogeneous sources as described in a number of papers by H. Peyton Young (2004, 2005, 2007), then one can express (6.24) as

$$dn = \alpha n \Delta N dt + \beta \Delta N dt = (\alpha n + \beta)\Delta N dt, \beta \geq 0. \tag{6.26}$$

From (6.26) the rate of diffusion is

$$\frac{dn}{dt} = (\alpha n + \beta)\Delta N \Rightarrow dn = (\alpha n + \beta)\Delta N dt \tag{6.27}$$

By variable separation,

$$\int \frac{dn}{(n+\theta)\Delta N} = \int \alpha dt, \theta = \frac{\beta}{\alpha}. \tag{6.28}$$

Upon partial differentiation

$$\frac{1}{n+\theta} \int \left(\frac{1}{N+\theta} + \frac{1}{\Delta N} \right) dn = A + \alpha t. \tag{6.29}$$

Assuming n(0) = 1, the cumulative number of adopters from more than one source is approximately

$$n = \frac{(\alpha+\beta) N e^{(\alpha N+\beta)t} - v(N-1)}{(N-1)\alpha + (\alpha+\beta) e^{(\alpha N+\beta)t}}. \tag{6.30}$$

Equation (6.30) is a logistic model that accounts for heterogeneous sources of learning, and hence adoption of innovations (Urban and Hauser 1981). It is the equivalent of H. Peyton Young's (2004) Equation 14 (p. 13). However, it is too orderly in structure, which preordains its predictions. In a creative reinterpretation of Rogers (1983, 2003), Barbara Wejnert (2002) provides a conceptual integration of three components of comprehensive models of the diffusion of innovations that stand in the way of such model orderliness: "Characteristics of innovations"; "characteristics of innovators"; and the "environmental context."

The first component concerns mainly financial and economic factors; the second focuses on the socioeconomy of innovations, and the third on the geography of innovations. All three components are potential sources and sinks of innovations. For example, when innovations have larger private benefits than private costs, they are likely to be adopted quickly, but spread slowly given such things as the protection of property rights. Pure public innovations are nonrival and nonexcludable; their rates of adoption and spread are largely a function of the political process, and its institutions. For instance, in a traditional economy the adoption and spread of innovations that increase productivity but reduce social security (perhaps by reducing social status and risking social disorder, real or perceived), will be slow. The influence of geography on the diffusion of innovations is a common subject of analysis among economists of growth and change. Not too long ago, the stress was on the (in)appropriateness of intermediate technologies to developing countries—a subject that, then as now, has strained the relations between developing countries on one hand, and multinational corporations in developed countries on the other hand. Today similar emphasis goes into the analysis of the externalities of clubs, trading blocs, networks, neighborhoods, and the like. This all indicates that Wejnert's framework is consistent with Fagerberg, Srholec, and Knell's (2007) argument that the spread of innovations is a function of many variables, including the technical capacity of adopters (cf. Drucker 1985). Technical capacity depends largely on economic factors like demand and price, in Fagerberg, Srholec, and Knell's analysis. Thus, current diffusion models are deficient to the extent that most of them compress the learning, and adoption dimensions of diffusion into one dimension whose success is measured in revealed use. Paradoxically, in real life success is seldom a good guide to progress. Mathematicians Springer, Herlihy, Mall, and Beggs (1968) point out that

> there is nothing very secret about success. Failures are the real secrets. As individuals we learn a lot more from our disappointments and failures than from success. . . . Learning seems to come from successive elimination of the causes for failure. From this point of view, nothing fails like success. (272–273)

Innovations Spread Like Wild Fire—Again

It is true that we do not know learning has taken place until adoption is complete. We do not know adoption is complete until we see the innovation in use. However, the Marx-Schumpeter's "gale of creative destruction" guarantees that what is in use is sooner or later discarded. In reality diffusion takes place in economic time determined by market forces and distributed in discrete units and over discrete time units. There are lags involved; one may learn in year t, but adopt in year t+j >> t. One also may adopt in year t+j, and still chose not to "share," or even quit that same year. In situations where successful use is preceded by many failures, the rate of spread of innovations is surely underestimated. This all suggests the need to modify (6.30*) to allow for social learning behavior of the type described in Young (ib.), as well as the wildfire-like phenomenon. In such cases the number of spreaders, adjusted for wildfire-like unpredictable behavior, is

$$n^* = R(t)n, R(t) = \frac{\Omega(1+\Psi)}{\mu}, \tag{6.31}$$

where R(t) is Rothermel's parameter of the spread of wildfire. While (6.30) is logistic, in (6.31) R(t) may be distributed differently. Let's assume R(t) is a Gompertz so that (6.31) becomes

$$n^* = n\left(e^{\lambda-\zeta\gamma^t}\right)\left[\frac{(\alpha+\beta)N e^{(\alpha N+\beta)t} - v(N-1)}{(N-1)\alpha + (\alpha+\beta)e^{(\alpha N+\beta)t}}\right]. \tag{6.32}$$

Since $n = n^* / R$, (6.32) = (6.30) iff R = 1. R = 1 requires e^0, which in turn requires $e^{\lambda-\zeta\gamma^t} = 0$, which is not possible because e > 0. Thus, according to (6.32) innovations spread like wildfire in that R is subject to the local forces of mutual propagation and inhibition.

If n(t) is inhibited (exhibited) by I—the ratio of the rate of resource consumption in the process of diffusion (learning, adoption, adaptation), to the capacity utilization rate (I)—that is,

$$\frac{\textit{Resource consumption rate}}{\textit{Capacity utilization rate}} \equiv \frac{\eta n^* + \rho n_1^*}{n^*},\ n_1^* = \frac{dn^8}{dt}, \tag{6.33}$$

then the rate of the spread of innovation would be

$$n^{***} = \frac{\xi n^* - \xi\eta n^* + \xi\rho n_1^*}{n^*} = \frac{Rn\xi - \xi\eta Rn + \xi\rho n_1^*}{Rn}. \tag{6.34}$$

Adjusting (6.32) for inhibitions (exhibitions) as well as wildfire-like behavior yields

$$n = \frac{\left(\xi\rho n_1^*\right)}{\xi(1-\eta)R} = \frac{\left(\xi\rho n_1^*\right)}{\xi(1-\eta)e^{\lambda-\zeta\gamma^z}}. \tag{6.35}$$

This means that (6.32) simplifies to

$$n^* = \frac{\xi\rho n_1^*}{\xi(1-\eta)}. \tag{6.36}$$

Equations (6.35) and (6.36) are economically informative. To see how, from (6.35) define $\tau = \xi\rho$ and $\pi = \xi(1-\eta)$. Since

$$n_1^* = \frac{dn^*}{dt} \text{ and } \frac{dn_1^*}{dt} = \frac{d^2n}{dt^2},$$

making necessary substitutions gives us

$$\frac{dn}{dt} = [\xi\rho(n_1^* - \zeta\gamma^t \ln\gamma)] / \xi(1-\eta)e^{\lambda-\zeta\gamma^t}. \tag{6.37}$$

Given the differential of (6.37) and solving (6.41) for the cumulative number of adopters yields

$$n = \int dn = \int \frac{[\xi\rho\left(1-\zeta\gamma^{t}ln\gamma\right]}{\left[\xi\left(1-\eta\right)e^{\lambda-\zeta\gamma^{t}}\right]}dt \qquad (6.38)$$

This shows that (6.27), (6.30), (6.35), and (6.38) cannot be the same, as each treat *n*, dn/dt, and dn differntly. However, (6.38) is a preferable generalization of which the other three are special cases.

CONCLUDING REMARKS

Appropriately modified logistic models continue to be useful tools for describing the spread of innovations. Generally logistic regression techniques such as the Logit technique, are nearly indispensable in assessing the loglikelihood of some economic event. Where repeated sampling is possible and learning processes can be modeled, logistic models have few competitors in predicting probable behaviors of economic variables. Their flexible lognormal distributions give them an additional advantage that captures varying rates of innovation spreads. Moreover, a logistic model can be transformed into a Gompertz, and into a modified exponential model of which both are family members. However, the benefit of flexibility is often purchased with too strong a currency, so to speak, in terms of the assumption about the tight structure that permits diffusion to proceed first at a slow rate, then at a fast rate, and eventually at an asymptotically declining rate.

In reality, the spread of an innovation is more complex than a simple logistic model predicts. A lot of institutional constraints and prospects are involved. Characterizing the constraints and prospects are individual behavioral interactions of many infrastructural and super-structural elements. The interactions determine the spread of innovations in dynamic, perhaps even chaotic, ways. In this chapter, one argument is that innovations spread more like wild fire than like systematic epidemics. This is no wild and speculative analogy; some environments are more susceptible to catching fire than others. Just as the rate of the spread of fire is a function of fuel and other factors, so too is the spread of innovations, only that in the latter case the fuel is human population. Human population is a necessary fodder for the spread of innovations. The sufficient condition is the quality of the human population which can favor or disfavor the spread of innovations, which explains why there are some random chances of finding islands untouched by fire surrounded by a sea of fire devastation, to continue the analogy.

Social learning can speed up or slow down the spread of innovations depending on how the population perceives Young's benefit/cost (payoff) matrix. However, social learning makes the spread of innovations less predictable. This calls for more realistic modifications to the logistic model, because traditional models of the spread of innovations such as (6.27) assume a homogeneous source of learning about innovations so that diffusion follows a neat logistic curve. Although such a rationalization is possible, it is highly improbably in a multimedia world. Adopters of innovations may not even know (remember) which of the many sources they learned an innovation from. Since learning itself is a cumulative process anyway, the last straw alone does not break the camel's back.

Adjusting (6.27) for social learning from heterogeneous sources adds a considerable degree of dynamism as well as realism to the process—resulting in (6.30). If the social and private payoffs are equal, the equilibrium rate of social learning drives the equilibrium rates of adoption and diffusion. Away from this equilibrium, nothing obvious suggests why and if (6.30*) should be logistic empirically. For one, innovations are always associated with externalities. If the marginal social benefits of an innovation outweigh the marginal private benefits, private markets of innovations will under-produce innovations.

This raises the need to either produce innovations by public means (subsidize supply or voucher demand), or live with the inefficient cost of underproduction. Second, if the marginal social cost is higher than the private marginal cost of an innovation, overproduction is the consequence, with further implications for the correction of negative externalities.

In either case, solutions away from the equilibrium are ambiguous. More likely than not innovations would spread in unpredictable ways, even across homogeneous populations, justifying the need to modify the social-learning model for unpredictable behavior. One can accommodate unpredictable behavior with a simple hypothesis that innovations spread like wildfires. For example, assuming that R(t) is a well-behaved (differentiable) function with a solution $0 \leq R^*(t) \leq +1$, then (6.30*) is logistic only in the neighborhood of +1. Above and below R*(t), not only does it scale up or down the spread, it also makes it fluctuate wildly like fire. This occurs not so much because the population is heterogeneous, but more so because of the specific and diverse characteristics as Barbara Wejnert (2002) suggests (cf. Bulliet 2002).

An additional complication is that, while *n* may be logistic, R(t) may be a Gompertz, for instance. It is true that the derivative of a Gompertz belongs to the same family of modified expontial functions as the logistic model (Banerjee 2007; Harris 1992; Thompson 1992). However, that does not mean the two are the same—not all twins are identical twins. Thus, like wildfires innovations spread in unpredictable ways. Underlying this behavior are systematic and systemic inhibitions and exhibitions. In that case, the final solution to the diffusion process would depend on the interactions between the forces that promote and those that subjugate the spread of innovations. As Wejnert (2002) put it,

> The broad array of diffusion variables . . . exert their effects on the process of diffusion interactively. The interaction between variables can be either potentiating or mitigating, and the relative weight of each variable may change according to the circumstances characterizing the innovation and its context. (p. 318)

Under such conditions it is no longer clear whether or not the logistic model is still an accurate description of the diffusion process. What is clear is that when the forces of promotion are stronger than the forces of subjugation, the capacity of the population to adopt and diffuse an innovation increases; when the opposite prevails, as the bee example illustrates, the innovation process is seriously complicated. In such situations understanding of the individual characteristics of the entire diffusion process is essential. What all this says for African countries is that

- they should not waste resources trying to reinvent wheels that already exist;
- they should resist the temptation to straight jacket innovation process; and
- they should prepare their populations (fodder) to catch and spread innovations easily.

These are areas for considerable future research interest.

NOTES

1. This assumption ignores that with modern technologies diffusion might not require involvement of progressively more people because one person can get to thousands of people in a click of a button.
2. I define diffusion as repeated and continuous adoption, with or without adaptation.
3. I use the word "die" in the broadest possible sense to mean loss of optimal functionality, and it would include biological death as well as things like forgetting and disability.
4. I assume a replacement birth rate for simplicity.

Chapter 7

Resource Intra- and Inter-actions

Implications for Technological Change and Economic Performance

The distinction between factors *and* forces *of production according to W. Arthur Lewis, and between* objects *and* ideas *according to Paul Romer is central to economic growth rate differences across economies, both have enriched economic growth theory. However, the distinction does not make explicit intra-actions among objects and ideas on the one hand, and the inter-actions among objects and ideas on the other hand. This analysis shows that resource intra-actions and inter-actions are important to technological change, and hence to economic growth. Economies with strong positive resource intra- and inter-actions produce more output than others. In fact, conceptually intra- and inter-active economies are characterized by economies of scale and produce twice as much output as others, and their rates of growth and change are high because of it. While how useful this analysis can be to policy is left to empirical investigations, theoretically SSACs will do well if they invested in resource inter- and intra-actions.*

To facilitate the transfer and spread of innovations, any economy requires recognition and exploitation of resource intra-actions and interactions as these are crucial to technological change and economic performance. This is no new idea; growth and change economists, irrespective of their philosophical and methodological orientations, generally agree on the fundamental rule of production: Output (y) is a function of productive resources commonly known as inputs or factors of production (X). While disagreements about the specific form of a production function and the importance of individual resources abound, there is little dispute about the list of productive resources: Labor (L), human capital (H), physical capital (K), land (R), and entrepreneurship (E). Given the list, classical economists have argued that output depends mainly on labor, at least in the short run. An important reason for their argument was that land came in limited supply, while physical capital was scarce, rudimentary, and perhaps even less productive than labor and land, and its rate of accumulation could reasonably be assumed constant. Adam Smith's (1976 [1776], Book II) discussion of the fixed and variable components of capital is interesting. However, in his outline of the "law of accumulation" and the "law of population" as drivers of economic growth, capital accumulation led to wage improvement with a lag of 15–25 years (Angresano 1992). But even then the wage increase was a temporary one and soon reversed by the growth of population. This suggests that capital was not considered particularly important to Smith's economy. Thus, it is not hard to understand how good economic thinking led Smith to the division of labor theory that excluded other factors of production, or how Malthus saw disaster in population growth (cf. Thompson 1992, Chapter III).

Ricardo accepted that the supply of land was limited, but land itself comes in varying grades of quality such that the supply of land, narrowly defined, is not perfectly inelastic with respect to its own price (rent). This innovation around the Malthusian scare of population growth demonstrated that scarcity is relative; it also formalized the classical overemphasis on the value of labor in production. Karl Marx (1906) noticed that capital and capital accumulation are both dynamic, but he too was in the end trapped in the "labor theory of value" so that $y = f(\mathrm{Re}\,sources) = f(X) = f(L \mid \bar{R}, K)$, where the vertical line means "on condition that" land is fixed (overbar) and capital, whatever amount, is given (hat).

For a while, labor and capital were considered the factors of production until Frank Knight (1921) and Joseph Schumpeter (1954, 2005) extended analysis to include the role of entrepreneurship (E) in y and y-growth (cf. Benjamin Higgins 1968, Part 2). From this general literature one can infer that economists have tended to divide resources (X) into factors (X_1) and forces (X_2) without saying so explicitly (Amavilah 1998; Amavilah and Newcomb 2004). For example, in a neoclassical fashion, Solow (1956, 1957) and Swan (1956, 2000) represent forces as (exogenous) technical change and factors as the conventional means of production (to use Marx's language). Sir W. Arthur Lewis (1965), a new classical, retains the conventional list of the factors of production and adds to it production forces: (a) "the will to economize," (b) economic institutions, (c) government, and (d) public policy, so that $y = f(\mathrm{Re}\,sources) = f(Factors, Forces) = f(X_1, X_2)$. However, this Lewis's fundamental innovation went completely unsung mainly because many economists know Lewis only through the narrow lens of his "development with unlimited supply of labor" (Lewis 1954).[1] A clear and emphatic statement of the distinction between factors (X_1) and forces (X_2) of production emerged for the first time from Paul Romer's (1993) insightful object-idea gaps.[2] See excellent overviews of new growth theories by Mark Rogers (2003) and Nazrul Islam (2004).[3]

The objective of this chapter is to restate the Lewis-Romer model in a simple and practical way by making as explicit as possible resource intra-actions and inter-actions. The restatement shows that resource intra-actions and inter-actions are critical to technological change and through it they explain level and growth rate differences across economies. The next section outlines resource intra-actions and inter-actions. The third section indicates that the intra-actions and inter-actions determine technological change. The fourth section places technological change at the center of economic growth and is followed by the fifth section which describes key variables that would allow empirical tests of the model, and proposes the road ahead.

RESOURCE INTRA-ACTIONS AND INTER-ACTIONS

Assuming an ideal economic universe (U), figure 7.1 describes how the black-box *f* transforms resources into *y*, and how post-production functions Φ (packaging, marketing, storage, etc.) add value to *y*, thereby affecting wealth (and welfare) which in turn influences the quality and quantity of resources. Positive changes in the quantity and quality of resources shift the production possibilities frontier outward thereby enlarge production possibilities and consumption possibilities. How fast growth is, and whether or not it is

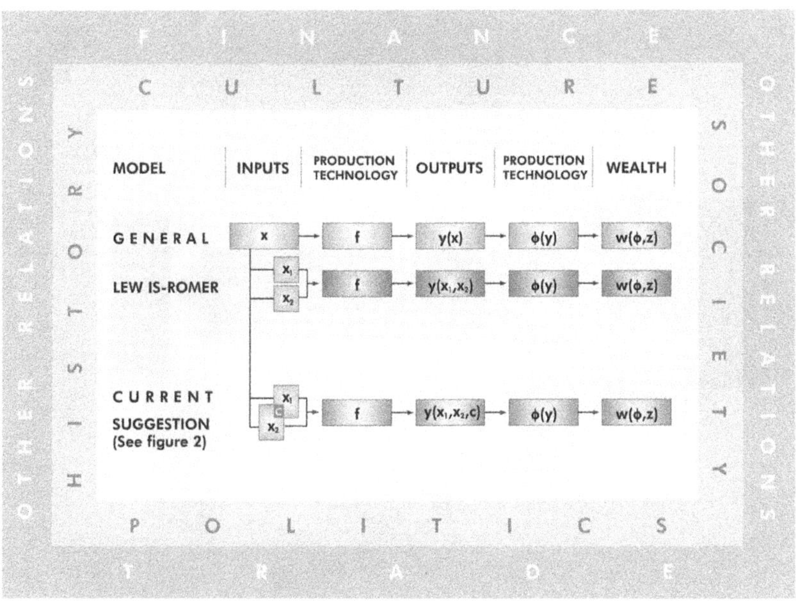

Figure 7.1 Basic Production Function Approaches. *Source*: Author.

sustainable, must recognize that the production process is a social process insofar as it is surrounded by all kinds of internal environments, some of which are economic, such as the economic system, others of which are political, such as democratic institutions, and still other of which are cultural, religious, what have you (Marx 1973; Max 1958, 1947; Polanyi 1957). Moreover, under resource globalization (localization) these internal environments are themselves affected by other external environments via international trade, finance, and other relations.

Now, assume that the economic universe (U) in figure 7.1 consists of two sub-universes U_1 and U_2, that is, $U = U_1 \cup U_2$. U_1 produces output y_1 using Romer's objects or Lewis's specialized factors (X_1). U_2 produces y_2 utilizing Romer's ideas or Lewis's forces (X_2). Also suppose there are interdependencies (1) among objects and ideas within each sub-universe, and (2) between objects and ideas across the two sub-universes of one universe. Call the former resource intra-actions, and the latter resource inter-actions. From figure 7.2 it should be clear that if $U = U_1 \Rightarrow U_2 = 0, C = 0$, then $y_1 = f(L_1^*, K_1^*, R_1^*; A)$, where $X^* = X - A$, and $A = L_1 \cap K_1 \cap R_1 \equiv \tau_1$ are object intra-actions representing object-embodied technological change. Similarly, for $X^* = X - B$, $y2 = f(L_2^*, K_2^*, R_2^*; B), B = L_2 \cap K_2 \cap R_2 \equiv \tau_2$ is technological change associated with idea intra-actions. Then the resource tie-bar between the two

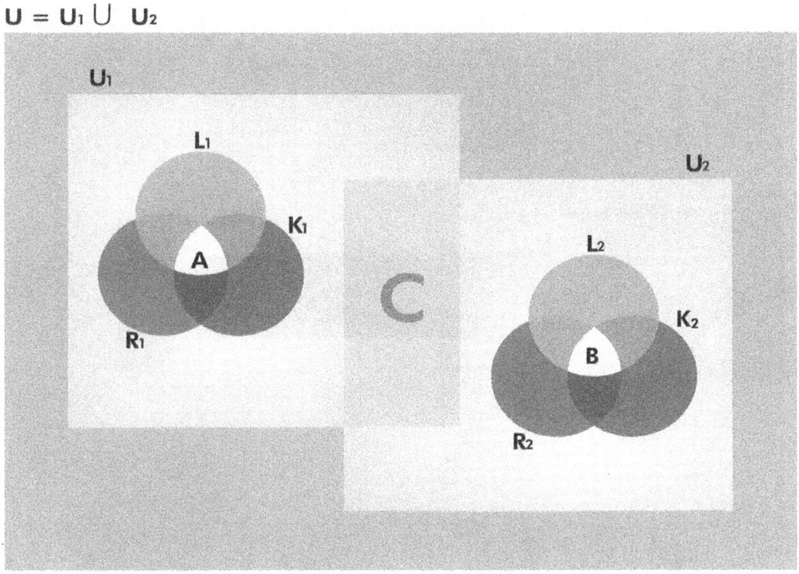

Figure 7.2 Resource Intra-actions and Interactions. *Source*: Author.

sub-universes are object-idea inter-actions, $C = U_1 \cap U_2 \equiv \tau_3$, signifying cross-universe technological change such that

$$y = (y_1 y_2)e^{C\equiv\tau} = \left[f\left(L_1^*, K_1^*, R_1^*, A \equiv \tau_1\right)g\left(L_2^*, K_2^*, R_2^*, A \equiv \tau_2\right)\right]e^{\tau_3}. \quad (7.1)$$

Now, giving (7.1) a Cobb-Douglass form produces

$$y = \left(L_1^{*\alpha_1} K_1^{*\beta_1} R_1^{*\gamma_1}\right)\left(L_2^{*\alpha_2} K_2^{*\beta_2} R_2^{*\gamma_2}\right)e^{\tau_1+\tau_2+\tau_3}. \quad (7.2)$$

where L_i, K_i, and R_i are labor, capital, and land, respectively. And since the limit of the sum of a dummy variable $\tau(x)$ is its integral, we can write

$$e^T = e^{\tau_1+\tau_2+\tau_3} = e^{\int\tau(x)dx}, \quad (7.3)$$

such that in general

$$y = \left[X_1^{\alpha_1} X_2^{\alpha_2}\right]e^{\int\tau(x)dx} = \left[X_1^{\alpha_1} X_2^{\alpha_2}\right]e^{\int T(x)+C}, \quad (7.4)$$

which resembles, but is not identical to, Romer's (1990) Y on p. S76-S77). Taking the natural logarithms of both sides of (7.4) above gives

$$lny = \alpha_1 \ln X_1 + \alpha_2 lnX_2 + \int\tau(x)dx = \alpha_1 \ln X_1 + \alpha_2 \ln X_2 + \int T(x) + C.$$

Given (7.5), average object- productivity and idea-productivity are

$$lny^* = \alpha_2 lnx_2 + [\int\tau(x)dx - \ln x_1],\ y^* = y / X_1,\ x_2 = \frac{X_2}{X_1} \quad (7.6a)$$

$$lny^* = \alpha_1 lnx_1 + [\int\tau(x)dx - \ln x_2],\ y^* = y / X_2,\ x_1 = \frac{X_1}{X_2}. \quad (7.6b)$$

INTRA-ACTIVE AND INTER-ACTIVE TECHNOLOGICAL CHANGE

Because

$$e^{\int\tau(x)dx} = e^{T(x)+C},\ \frac{d}{dx}\left[e^{T(x)+C}\right] = \tau(x) \Rightarrow d\left[e^{T(x)+C}\right] = \tau(x)dx,$$

it follows that partial differentiation of (7.4) give resource elasticities as

$$\xi_{x_i} \equiv (\partial \ln y)/(\partial \ln X_i) = a_i + e^{\tau_i(x)}\Delta\tau(x) = 0, \Delta\tau(x) = \frac{d\tau(x)}{dX}, i = 1,2 \qquad (7.7a)$$

$$\xi_{\tau_1(x)} \equiv \frac{lny}{\partial\tau_1(x)} = e^{\int\tau(x)dx}[1 + \Delta\tau_1(x)] = 0 \Rightarrow \Delta\tau_1(x) = [d\tau(x)dX]e^{\int\tau(x)dx} \qquad (7.7b)$$

$$\xi_{\tau_2(x)} \equiv \frac{lny}{\partial\tau_2(x)} = (\Delta\tau_2(x))^2 = 0 \Rightarrow \Delta\tau_2(x) = [\tau(x)dX]e^{\int\tau(x)dx} \qquad (7.7c)$$

$$\xi_{\tau(x)} \equiv \frac{\partial lny}{\partial\tau(x)} = \Delta\tau(x)\left[e^{\tau_1(x)+\tau_2(x)}\right] \qquad (7.7d)$$

In (7.7) note that X_i are non-stochastic (exogenous) while $\tau_i\,(x)$ are stochastic so that $\int$ disappears in the former but not in the latter. So, setting $\partial \ln y / \partial \ln x_i = \partial \ln y / \partial\tau_i(x) = 0$ and solving for $\tau_i\,(x)$ leads to

$$\tau_1(x) = \ln\left[\frac{(1 + \Delta\tau(x))e^{\int\tau(x)dx} - a_1}{\Delta\tau(x)}\right] \qquad (7.8a)$$

$$\tau_2(x) = \ln\left[\frac{(\Delta\tau_1(x))^2 - a_2}{\Delta\tau(x)}\right] \qquad (7.8b)$$

With (7.5) and (7.6) in hand we can find the composite technology (e^T) as $e^T = \int\tau(x)dx.$

Note that (7.8) seems to indicate that the resources of U_2 (ideas) are not important determinants of technological change. Not so, the expression only appears that way because deriving τ_1 (x) assumed τ_2 (x) is constant and vice versa. In truth $\tau_2(x) = f(\Delta\tau_1(x), a_2) \Rightarrow \tau(x) = f(\tau_i(x), a_i)$. In fact, $\tau_3(x) = \tau(x) - \tau_1(x) - \tau_2(x)$. Hence, given τ(x) it is a matter of standard theory to obtain the level of X_i^* associated with a given level of isoquant y^0—that is not so hard to do. What is challenging to demonstrate is the shape of the isoquant given a shifting τ(x)—but the assertion is a separate investigation altogether. Also unique here is that setting $\xi_{X_1} = \xi_{X_2} = 0$ and solving for $\Delta\tau(x)$ gives

$$\Delta\tau(x) = \frac{a_1 - a_2}{e^{\tau_1(x) - \tau_2(x)}} = \frac{MP_{X_1}^0 - MP_{X_2}^0}{e^{\tau_1(x) - \tau_2(x)}} \tag{7.9}$$

where MP_i^0 are conventional marginal products, and $\Delta\tau(x)$ is technological change associated with crossing universes from U_1 to U_2. These types of technological shifts are described in Amavilah (1998) and Amavilah and Newcomb (2004). They suggest that moving to one universal state requires abandoning another altogether. This was indeed the early understanding of the industrialization process where an economy moves out of agriculture and mining into manufacturing and then into services, leaving behind a better standard of living on average along with ghost mining towns, for example, as interactive linkages between universes first weaken and eventually disappear. Of course, this result is not entirely improbable (see Amavilah 2005).

In the present case linkages need not weaken; MP_i are variable, that is,

$$MP_{X_i} = \frac{y^* \xi_{X_i}}{X_i} = X_j^{a_j}]e^{\int \tau(x)dx} \tag{7.10}$$

Hence, the variable intra-universal and inter-universal marginal rates of resource transformation can be approximated by

$$\lambda_{\{ij\}} = \xi x_i, \xi = \frac{\xi_{X_i}}{\xi_{X_j}} . x_i = \frac{X_i}{X_j}, \tag{7.11}$$

and intra-resource and inter-resource elasticities of substitution (η) are roughly

$$\eta = \xi \frac{dx}{d\lambda}. \tag{7.12}$$

Note that (7.11) and (7.12) are mathematically vague; whereas tuition demands clarity, intuition permits vagueness as a substitute for flexibility because while X_2 may be a close substitute for or complement of X_1, X_1 can be a poor substitute for X_2 but just as a good complement. Example: in the operating room, a medical technician (labor) while a good complement is not a close substitute for a surgeon (human capital). Moreover, because ξ_{Xi} are variable, careful calculations show variable scale elasticity as

$$\varepsilon = \xi_{X_1} + \xi_{X_2} + \xi_\tau = \left[a_1 + a_2 + 2\Delta\tau(x)\right] e^{\tau_1(x) + \tau_2(x)} \tag{7.13}$$

Eq. (7.13) clearly suggests that intra-active and inter-active economies are subject to increasing returns to scale, because even if $a_1 + a_2 < 1$, $\forall\ \tau_i(x) \geq 0, \frac{d^2}{dx^2} e^{\tau_i(x)} > 0, \ni \varepsilon \geq 1$.

ECONOMIC GROWTH WITH INTRA-ACTIVE AND INTER-ACTIVE TECHNOLOGICAL CHANGE

Differentiating (7.4) with respect to time gives the proportionate growth rate. Disregarding resource intra- and inter-actions, however,

$$\dot{y} = a_1 \dot{x}_1 + a_2 \dot{x}_2 + a_0 \tag{7.14}$$

where a_0 is either Hicks-Solow, Harrod-Domar neutral rate of technical change (Thirlwall 1978; Choi 1983), or Verdoorn-Arrow learning effect (Arrow 1962), and the dot indicates the growth rate of the variable over which it stands. Considering resource intra- and inter-actions

$$\dot{y} = \xi_1 \dot{x}_1 + \xi_2 \dot{x}_2 + \xi_\tau \left(\tau \equiv a_0\right) \tag{7.14'}$$

So, asks Hall and Jones (1999), "why do some countries produce so much more output per worker than others?" Part of the answer is: because some economies have stronger resource intra- and inter-actions than others and are therefore predisposed to economies of scale. In fact, intra- and inter-active economies would produce twice as much output as others, and their rates of growth are high because of it.

CONCLUDING REMARKS: WHERE TO FROM HERE?

Paul Romer's notion of idea and object gaps as constraints on economic growth has enriched economic growth theory enormously! So did WA Lewis's division of productive resources into factors and forces. Although Romer acknowledges important interactions involving the flow of ideas between developing and industrialized countries via multinational corporations, both Romer and Lewis are not explicit about intra- and inter-actions among factors that are essential to technological change. In their extension of Romer, Graca, Jafarey, and Philippopoulos (1995) characterize interactions between human capital (idea) and physical capital (object) in an endogenous framework.[4] The results of their characterization indicate that dynamic economic growth depends increasingly on ideas as the level of development increases. By extension, the brief analysis of this essay argues for intra-actions among objects and ideas on the one side, and inter-actions among objects and ideas on the other hand. Then technological change becomes the integrand of these resource intra- and inter-actions. From this narrow viewpoint, economies with strong resource intra- and inter-actions produce more output than others, and their growth rates are better because of it. Romer (undated) is correct "that economic growth springs from better recipes, not just from more cooking" (page 2 of 5) or different cooks. This is a powerful distinction, for it tells us to be careful about how we account for human capital and its implications for both technological change and economic growth. For example, as a human capital Albert Einstein is really two different Einsteins in the Romer-Lewis model of economic growth. The first Albert Einstein is the brilliant scientist with wild hair. This Einstein, like an expensive machine, is an object. The second Albert Einstein is an idea (e.g., $E = MC^2$)—a recipe. Although Professor Einstein (object) is the originator of Einstein (idea = formula), the Idea Einstein is now independent of the Object Einstein. Like a machine when Professor Object Einstein passed away, his marginal product fell to zero. The same cannot be said of Professor Idea Einstein, because there the marginal product may actually be rising with improvement and applications of the formula. Again, Professor Adam Smith is long gone; his conception of a capitalist economy is in fact stronger and more widely spread than it was during his lifetime.

Back to Romer's cooking example again. The rate of growth and quality of the growth of the output of a fruitcake depend on the intra-actions among objects (ingredients), ideas (recipes), as well as the interactions among recipes and ingredients. Another shot: in a traditional economy, successful hunting requires that a hunter (primary object), and his/her bow and arrow (intermediate objects) intra-act with one another, as well as inter-act with the hunter's knowledge of hunting (idea). Modern objects, ideas, and their accumulation via investment are more sophisticated than what "primitive" hunting requires. However, the production process is essentially the same, differing only in the ratios of object-object and idea-idea intra-actions, on the one side, and object-idea inter-actions on the other side. Many countries and their advisers like the World Bank and IMF have gotten better at managing object-object production relations. Also many countries are on their way to understanding object-idea relations, and those are doing well now. *The gap among nations in performance is about idea-idea production relations, and that is the future.* The policy implications of this essay may be premature, but it is not unreasonable to assert that an obvious research implication is that any model that overlooks resource intra-actions and interaction underutilizes powerful aspects of endogenous growth theory.

For now one may ask: What are the necessary variables and where does one find the data for them in order to implement these ideas? This is a good question, and like all good questions also a difficult one. However, chief among the objects (X_1), both Lewis and Romer would include fixed and intermediate inputs, such as "raw" labor (L_1), fixed capital LESS depreciation (K_1), and land (R_1) in the classical sense of "gift of Nature"—or is it "nature"? The intra-actions among these "classical, original" inputs represent (a Solow-like) technological change (τ_1). Ideas or forces would include human capital ($L_2 \equiv H$) first and foremost. Second, they would include what Taylor (2000) calls fluid capital PLUS depreciation (K_2) according to Hotelling (1925), and finally they would include enhanced land and other natural resources (R_2). The difference between R_1 and R_2 is that the former refers to land as a piece of earth on which a factory building stands, for example; the latter would include processed and semi-processed commodities such as cut and polished versus rough diamonds, ex-situ vis-a-vis in-situ crude oil, or tanned leather as opposed to rawhide or even a live cow, for instance. The intra-actions among these "classical reproducible, derived, secondary, or higher" inputs produce a second variety of technological change (τ_2).[5] Quite obviously, goods and services are neither purely object-based nor purely idea-based. For example, some computer components are best produced where the costs of objects are lowest, others where ideas are predominant and cost may be of secondary consideration, and still other computer parts require a good mix of ideas and objects to produce. Inter-actions among objects and ideas lead to a third technological change (τ_3), so that overall technological change (T) is the sum, and in the limit the integral, of the three technological changes. Then Solow's technical progress (at least as interpreted by Abramovitz 1979) is T + random error term.

What the preceding statements show is that the problem in implementing the modified Lewis-Romer scheme outlined here is not about the lack of clarity of variable definitions and unavailability of data. Neither is it due to the absence of economies sufficiently intra-active and inter-active to allow for study examples. Cesar Hidalgo and Ricardo Hausmann (2009) have shown that precisely conceptualized even "economic complexity" can be easily explained. The problem is statistical. As Romer (1993) points out quantitative growth economists like the statistical convenience accorded by the assumptions of exogeneity—it make things easy; it is familiar; and it produces elegant results.

Yet I can think of at least one, albeit crude, alternative approach that would permit empirical estimations. First, one can employ a number of triple-variable correlation measures outlined by Pan and Harries (2000) to weed out meaningless and or other suspicious correlations. For instance, suppose after eliminating those correlations from the original set of variables the following is left:

$$y = (L_1K_1R_1)^a (L_2K_2R_2)^b (L_1K_2R_2)^c (K_1L_2R_2)^d (R_1L_2K_2)^e, \quad (7.15)$$

where *a*, *b*, *c*, *d*, and *e* are constants, and 1 and 2 indicate object-idea correlations on the basis of a Pan-Harris triple-variable correlation matrix (see pp. 134–37). For triply correlated variables *L*, *K*, and *R*, Pan and Harris define μ_L as the difference between actual *L* and average *L*, μ_K is the difference between *K* and average *K*, and μ_R is the difference between *R* and average *R*, and demonstrate that the correlation coefficient of a triplet LKR on a sample of *n* size is

$$\Theta_{LKR} = \left[\left(\sum_i^n (\mu) \right) \right] \Big/ \left[\sum_i^n (\mu^3) \right]^{\frac{1}{3}} \quad (7.16)$$

Equation (7.16) represents either area A, B, or C in figure 7.2 subject to the regularity, linearity and symmetry conditions (see Pan and Harris, ib., p. 134). Pan and Harris also detail other applicable measures such as the "generalized similarity coefficient" (p. 136) for quantitative triplets and the "extended match coefficient" (p. 149) for qualitative triplets. And so, given (7.15) the general production is now

$$y = f(L, K, R; \Theta_{LKR}) \quad (7.17)$$

Again, to reduce statistical hazards (7.17) faces, assume the following resource constraints:

$$L \equiv L_1^{a_1} L_2^{a_2} \Rightarrow \left(LL_2^{-a_2}\right)^{\frac{1}{a_1}};\ K \equiv K_1^{\beta_1} K_2^{\beta_2} \Rightarrow K_1 = \left(KK_2^{-\beta_2}\right)^{\frac{1}{\beta_1}};\ R \equiv R_1^{\gamma_1} R_2^{\gamma_2} \Rightarrow \left(RR_2^{-\gamma_2}\right)^{\frac{1}{\gamma_1}}.$$

Given those constraints we can now express (7.17) in terms of the intensity of ideas in aggregate labor and capital, which, dividing both sides by *L* (or any other variable of choice) to a familiar looking expression. However, careful analysis reveals that assuming intra-active and interactive triplets X_i, X_j, and X_k, dividing through (7.17) by $X_{i,}$ and taking the natural logs, technological change will be different from both the Solow-Swan and Romer traditions although based in them.

NOTES

1. I appreciate words of encouragement from Paul Romer, now Nobel Laurete for 2018, on an early draft of this essay, and the email conversation that developed with him and his colleague Brandon Fuller of Chatercities. I have been a fan of Paul's work since I first heard about it from Professor Irma Adelman, Professor Vernon Ruttan, and Professor Richard Bishop when they delivered Lectures in Economics at the University Graduate Faculty of Economics Lecture Series at Oregon State University at the invitation of the late Emery N. Castle (1988–1989). All mistakes are mine alone.

2. Lewis's book was first published in 1953 and his 1954 famous article is based on that book.

3. Volume 8, No. 1 of the *Journal of Economic Perspectives* (1994) carries a number of perspectives on economic growth by some of the outstanding growth and change economists including Paul Romer himself.

4. There is renewed interest in resource interactions see, for example, Philippe Aghion (2006), Chad I. Jones (2006), and Chad I. Jones and Paul Romer (2009), but no research on resource intra-actions.

5. The terms "classical, original" inputs and "classical reproducible, derived" inputs are either from or inspired by Samuelson (1994).

Conclusion

The preceding chapters were all written long before the Great Global Recession (GGR). All remain relevant, and some of them more so today than at the time they were written. Now it is natural to want to know the impact of the GGR on the performance of SSACs. While such a desire is understandable, and there may well be experts out there to address that need, generally speaking systematic and systemic analysis require available data to mature into relevant insights and knowledge.

What is clear instead is that many experts predicted terrible things to happen to SSACs as a result of the GGR. To date, given available information, there is no evidence that the impact of the GGR has been unique for SSACs. Mustapha Nabli (2010), for example, shows with ten case studies that the GGR has undermined the globalization process and hence economic growth world-wide. The ten countries studied were expected to decline by –6 percent to –8 percent by 2015, equivalently an Okun output gap of –7 percent. In practice, however, the net impact across countries turned out to be due in large part to differences in initial conditions, policy responses, and domestic aggregate demand. Specifically, while China, India, and Brazil appear least affected, the GGR hit East Asian countries hardest because of these countries' growth reliance on foreign trade (MA Weiss and VC Jones 2010). The direct effects of the GGR on SSACs have been mainly on foreign aid and remittances, a disguised blessing resulting from the fact that SSACs' share of global trade is relatively small, and in some other cases some SSACs enjoy liberal trade preferential with industrialized nations.

In his "Africa rocketing out of the recession," Keith Campbell (2010) credits the "resilient factor to good economic policy, especially flexible exchange rates, fiscal surpluses, and the China-Africa" link of late (Simons 2019). China's role will enhance Africa's position globally. However, it is also the case that much of China's dealings with SSACs are financial, and money is not a factor of production. Africa has long suffered from "odious debts," resulting in capital outflows and little investment (Ajayi and Ndikumana 2015; Boyce and Ndikumana 2001; Ndikumana and Boyce 2011) It is important to note that of the ten economies that shrank most during this recession, six were southern SSACs. This makes good sense because Southern African countries like Botswana, Namibia, and South Africa are more integrated in the global financial systems than other SSACs. The six West African economies that also declined significantly during the recessionary years were all Francophone countries, and thus closely linked to the European debt crises. That is the downside; the upside is that a few SSACs were on a successful trajectory before the GGR. In the cases of Botswana and Mauritius, James A. Robinson (2009) and A. Subramanian (2009), respectively, have argued that success there has institutional bases.

Sher Verick and I. Islam (2010) say that the financial crises was caused by lax government regulations in the industrialized countries, money policy, global imbalances, fickle financial and housing markets, and unsustainable household debt. Given that the GGR was really the sum of the financial crisis and economic crisis, it is now apparent that the financial crisis led to the economic crisis, and the GGR worsened as the commodity price boom ended and credit availability tightened. Even so, SSACs declined only from 6 percent to 2 percent and up to 4 percent, compared to negative growth in many industrialized countries. For example, of the 10 fastest growing countries during the 2008–2009 time period, three were African countries, and only two of the ten fastest declining countries were African. Cho and Newhouse (2011), using evidence from seventeen middle-income countries, observe different effects on "different types of workers." In South Africa the GGR hit aggregate growth hardest and affected largely wage (uneducated) workers, but unfortunately South Africa was the only SSAC in the study which makes it difficult to generalize the implications for all SSACs. Overall the SSA region, like other regions, is not out of the recessionary woods yet! Short-term, short-run dangers are still present. However, long-term, the long-run prospects favor this group of countries for the first time ever, so much so that Simons (2019) observes an "unsung industrial revolution" involving a new kind of transformation. Thus, while from the historical perspective the GGR will surely have valuable lessons for SSA, at the moment there is nothing I would change in these chapters as a result of that.

These chapters do not deal with the GGR and its effects on SSACs. Their singular goal is to promote the positive positive economics of the performance of SSACs in the decade just before the GGR by examining the factors and forces behind the recent economic performance of these countries. To accomplish the goal I set a number of manageable objectives and pursue them with six chapters, sandwiched between this conclusion and the preface. The first chapter quantifies the impact of the intensity of technology use on per capita real GDP of some SSACs. *Ceteris paribus*, it finds that technology has been a major constraint of the growth of African countries in general. However, the intensity of use of the internet and mobile phone positively explains the recent growth of real GDP per capita across the countries in the study sample. I conclude that these countries would benefit further from improved technology and increased distribution and use of internet and cell phone technologies. Generally speaking there would be no differences between other economists and me concerning the role of technology in the transformation of SSACs (Monga and Lin 2015a, b). However, I acknowledge that technological change affects different economies differently. This is the idea Takeda (2016) illustrates with the example of Japan, where positive macroeconomic effects of technology and trade influenced consumption behavior, and consumption increased welfare but only by destroying some industries. Since high consumption requires high production, the general environment was negatively affected thereby reducing welfare and rising social insecurity. These kinds of effects are likely magnified by the level of development, because while globalization and technological change tend to narrow the gap across countries (convergence), their benefits tend to go to high-income individuals in both developing and developed countries, and consequently raise within country inequality (divergence). SSACs are no exception to this phenomenon as Andres, Amavilah, and Asongu (2017) demonstrate.

Why is this happening this time after so many years of frustrations? Part of the answer is that the costs of initiating newer technologies are lower than those of adopting and spreading older technologies. *The main reason, however, is that the knowledge that now eases the transfer of newer technologies has been accumulating quietly in these countries as the example of the data from Botswana, Namibia, and South Africa illustrates.* The knowledge basis of technology is important to real GDP because it is important to technology. One may conclude that all SSACs would gain from increased investment in knowledge-building activities including publishing. This potential gain justifies further research on the topic.

To trace the specific sources of economic performance in these countries, I asked whether performance depends on domestic resources, global links, and or institutional quality. The results of the analysis confirm the significant role of gross investment, human capital, and openness to the global economy. However, the major source and hindrance of performance are the quality of institutions, measured by governance indices in which the rule of law and freedom of expression, safety and security, and human development constrain economic performance, while other factors promote it. The conclusion of fourth chapter agrees with that of fifth which uses a different index of globalization than openness to global trade and finance. For example, using a production function approach in which economic activity depends on measures of globalization, governance, and some controls, subsequent analysis finds that, besides physical and human capital and technical change, globalization, especially social globalization, is good for economic performance. These findings and my interpretation of them are consistent with Baldwin's (2017) in that globalization has had a positive global effect, including on Africa's economic performance. However, when we disaggregate globalization utilizing KOF data, the effects are mixed. Hence, what is convergence in the sense of "old globalization" is likely divergence in terms of the "new globalization," according to Baldwin (Ocampo, Jomo K.S., and Vos, 2007). Dani Rodrik (1997) has anticipated the limits to globalization and is now convinced globalization is paradoxical (2011).

A reviewer of the prepublication of the manuscript of this book brought to my attention a strand of literature that adds perspective to the "understanding of the international political economy of Africa's economic performance." Since the works he suggested are forward looking and likely provide a basis for future research, I think this is a good place to bring them up. Charnock and Starosta (2016), for example, observe that uneven development is a function of production relative to the surplus value of labor. While I acknowledge readily that there is more than one way of explaining performance, I am unwilling to engage a Marxian perspective. However, Sheppard (2016) is correct that there are disruptive limits to globalization. This is not a brand new idea; Krugman (1997) made an attempt to reintroduce economic geography into economic theory and to assess its implications for economic development. What I found consistent with my story here is the notion that capitalist performance depends on cultural geography and that geography reinforces social and spatial inequality, leading to poverty in some countries and wealth in others. The current bubble in nationalism and political protests points to the demand for "better information" to enable "quality decisions" for a "better society" (Sarokin and Schulkin, 2016).

The last two chapters of this book are theoretical; the common objective for them is to assess whether the recent performance is sustainable. Working from the premise that the technologies that African countries need to keep growing are available somewhere in the world, and that the transfer costs are lower than the innovation costs even with the advantage of imitation, the first of the last two chapters makes a modest correction to the existing literature on the spread of innovations. The correction emphasizes two points. First is the idea that innovations spread more like wildfire than like systematic epidemics. In that spread, the quality of the human population explains unequal distribution of innovations even within homogenous populations. Second, the rate at which innovations spread is subject to the forces of exhibition and inhibition, whereas exhibitors promote the spread of innovations and inhibitors subjugate it. Therefore, where the forces of subjugation are stronger than the forces of promotion, it is the slow spread, rather than the lack, of innovations which undermines the competitiveness of nations, and consequently frustrates economic performance. Then a general conclusion from the analysis is that SSACs should (a) not waste scarce resources trying to reinvent the wheels that already exist, (b) not succumb to the temptation to straightjacket innovation processes, and (c) prepare their populations (fodder) to catch and spread innovations easily, speaking figuratively.

The final chapter shows that resource intra-actions and inter-actions are important to technological change, and hence to economic performance. Economies with strong positive resource intra- and inter-actions produce more output than others. In fact, intra- and inter-active economies are characterized by economies of scale and would produce twice as much output as others, and their rates of growth are high because of it. How useful this analysis can be to policy is left to empirical investigations. Here, too, African countries, like other countries, should reflect in their policies the resource synergies with the potential to sustain their pre-GGR course of performance and permanently reverse the misfortunes that they have suffered over so many years.

How feasible are these proposals in the age of nationalism and global trade protectionism? Well, with all its limitations, especially international trade and finance as opposed to technology, globalization has generated significant gains for many around the world. The problem, and it is not a minor one, has been the unequal distribution of gains from globalization. Protectionism itself is not a new phenomenon; the so-called infant industry hypothesis was used to justify the import-substitution strategies of the 1950s and the neo-Marxist "unequal exchange" propositions of the 1960s and 1970s. The current atmosphere surrounding global trade protection is notable mainly because it involves the two largest economies in the world, in which one (USA) advocates for trade wars while the other (China) squeamishly vows retaliation. Of course, as an old African saying goes, "When two bull elephants fight, it is the grass beneath that suffers the most." That said, the reconsiderations of unions (e.g., Brexit), and trade agreements (e.g., NAFTA, Trans Pacific Trade Agreement, Paris Accord, etc.) question the benefits of legal oligopolies. Regarding SSACs in this respect, Mshomba's (2017) comparative analysis of the East African Economic Community's attempt at integration reveals opportunities as well as challenges. Now, will the Africa Continental Free Trade Area (AfCFTA) succeed where existing regional communities have not done so well? The answer is: It depends. If AfCFTA succeeds it will integrate 1.2 billion people, creating a US$4 trillion market economy. Signe (2017) estimates that such integration will increase intra-Africa trade by 53 percent, or twice that much if non-tariff barriers are zeroed out. Integration will allow the diversification of manufacturing and give rise to economies of both scale and scope to the tune of $6.7 trillion as a result of household and business consumption. These all should aid the ideas outlined in the preceding two chapters, except that initially the benefit will likely be uneven with most of it going to the African countries with large industrial foundations like South Africa, Kenya, and Egypt. However, I agree with Signe (2017) that even if AfCFTA fails, failure is an innovation because "development is problem-solving" (Nyarko 2007).

References

This section documents the works which guided my thoughts about the economic growth of SSACs as described here; it is neither exhaustive nor permanent as I reserve the right to change my mind. I hope the documentation acknowledges everyone directly cited in these chapters. If I missed anyone, or somehow failed to attribute ideas to whoever originated them, credit should go when credit is due. In all cases, and without exceptions and excuses, all errors are mine alone.

Abramovitz, M. 1986. "Catching Up, Forging Ahead, and Falling Behind." *Journal of Economic History* 46 (2): 385–406.

Abramovitz, M. 1979. "Rapid Growth Potential and Its Realization: The Experience of Capitalist Economies in the Postwar Period." In *Economic Growth and Resources*, edited by E. Malinvaud. New York: St. Martin's Press.

Acemoglu, D., S. Johnson, and J.A. Robinson. 2001a. "African Success Story: Botswana." MIT Department of Economics Working Paper No. 01-37.

Acemoglu, D., S. Johnson, and J.A. Robinson. 2001b. "The Colonial Origins of Comparative Development: An Empirical Investigation." *American Economic Review* 91 (5): 1369–1401.

Acemoglu, D., S. Johnson, and J.A. Robinson. 2002. "Reversal of Fortunes: Geography and Institutions in the Making of the Modern World Income Distribution." *Quarterly Journal of Economics* 117 (November): 1131–1295.

African Development Bank. 2009. "Africa Recovery/Renewal. 2003: Africa Economic Growth Falters." http://www.un.org/geninfo/afrec/newrels/ecaera.htm.

AfricanFocus. 2005. "Africa: Economic Growth Improving." http://www.africafocus.org/docs05/eca0505.php.

Aghion, P. 2006. "Interaction Effects in the Relationship between Growth and Finance." *Berkeley Electronic Press* 1 (1): Article 2. http://www.bepress.com/cas/vol1/iss1/art2.

Ajayi, S. and L. Ndikumana (eds). 2015. *Capital Flight from Africa: Causes, Effects, and Policy Issues*. New York: Oxford University Press.

Akerlof, G. 2007. "The Missing Motivations in Macroeconomics." *American Economic Review* 97 (1): 5–36.

Alcala, F. and A. Ciccone. 2001. "Trade and Productivity." IMF Working Paper (October).

Amavilah, V.H., A. Asongu, and A. Andres. 2017. "Effects of Globalization on Peace and Stability: Implications for Governance and the Knowledge Economy of African Countries." *Technological Forecasting and Social Change* 122 (C): 91–103.

Amavilah, V.H. 2008. *Modeling Income Determinants in Embedded Economies: Cross-Section Applications to U.S. Native American Economies*. New York: Nova Science Publishers, Inc.

Amavilah, V.H. 2004. "'Does Trade Cause Growth?'—A Comment." https://econwpa.ub.uni-muenchen.de/econ-wp/ge/papers/0307/0307001.pdf

Amavilah, V.H. 2006. "Institutional Change and Economic Performance: An Off-the-Cuff Comment on Professors Daron Acemoglu, Simon Johnson and James Robinson's Three Papers." http://ssrn.com/abstract=911324.

Amavilah, V.H. 1997[1996]. *Resources, Technology, and Mineral Trade in the Economic Growth of Namibia*, PhD Diss. Ann Arbor: UMI [University of Arizona].

Amavilah, V.H. 1998. "Resource Inefficiency and Poor Aggregate Economic Performance in African Countries: The Case of Namibia, 1968–1992." http://econpapers.repec.org/paper/wpawuwpdc/0307005.htm

Amavilah, V.H. and R.T. Newcomb. 2004. "Economic Growth and the Financial Economics of Capital Accumulation under Shifting Technological Change." http://econpapers.repec.org/paper/wpawuwpge/0404001.htm

Andrés, R., S.A. Asongu, and V.H. Amavilah. 2015. "The Impact of Formal Institutions on Knowledge Economy." *Journal of the Knowledge Economy* 6 (4): 1034–1062.

Andrés, A.R., V.H. Amavilah, and S.A. Asongu. 2017. "Linkages between Formal Institutions, ICT Adoption and Inclusive Human Hevelopment in Sub-Saharan Africa." In *Catalyzing Development through ICT Adoption*, edited by H. Kaur, E. Lechman, and A. Marszk. Springer: 175–203.

Angresano, J. 1992. *Comparative Economics*. Englewood Cliffs (NJ): Prentice Hall.

Archibugi, D. and A. Coco. 2005. "Measuring Technological Capabilities at the Country Level: A Survey and a Menu for Choice." *Research Policy* 34:175–194.

Arieff, A., M.A. Weiss, and V.C. Jones. 2010. "The Global Economic Crisis: Impact on Sub-Saharan African and Global Response. U.S. Congressional Research Service." www.fas.org/sgp/crs/nw/r40778.pdf.

Aron, J. 2000. "Growth and Institutions: A Review of Evidence." http://www.worldbank.org/research/journals/wbro/obsfeb00/Article_6.pdf (February).

Arora, V. and A. Vamvakidis. 2005. "The Implications of South Africa Economic Growth for the Rest of Africa." IMF Working Paper WP/05/58.

Arrow, K. 1962. "The Economic Implications of Learning by Doing." *Review of Economic Studies* 29: 155–173.

Arrow, K.J. 1969. "Classificatory Notes on the Production and Transmission of Technological Knowledge."*American Economic Review* 59 (2): 29–35.

Artadi, E.V. and X. Sala-i-Martin. 2003. "The Economic Tragedy of the XXth Century: Growth in Africa." NBER Working Paper No. 9865 (July).

Asongu, S., V. Amavilah, and A. Andres. 2019. "Business Dynamics, Knowledge Economy, and the Economic Performance of African Countries." *Information Development* 35 (5): 673–675.

Auty, Richard. 1993. *Sustaining Development in Mineral Economies: The Resource Curse Thesis*. London: Routledge.

Aziakpono, M.J. n.d. "Financial Development and Economic Growth in Southern Africa." Department of Economics, National University of Lesotho. https://www.oecd.org/dataoecd/38/12/30225204.pdf.

Baldwin, R. 2016. *The Great Convergence: Information Technology and the New Globalization*. Cambridge and London: Harvard University Press/Belknap Press.

Baltagi, B.H. 1999. *Econometrics*, 2nd revised edition. New York: Springer-Verlag, Chapter 12: 307–330.

Banerjee, A. 2007. "An Analysis of Logistic Models: Exponential Family Connections and Online Performance." http://www-users.cs.umn.edu/~banerjee/papers/07/logistic.pdf.

Barro, R. 1991. "Economic Growth in a Cross Section of Countries." *Quarterly Journal of Economics* CVI (2): 407–443.

Barro, R. and J-W. Lee. 2000. "International Data on Educational Attainment: Updates and Implications." CID Working Paper No. 42. http://www.cid.harvard.edu/cidwp/pdf/042.pdf (April).

Barro, R. and J-W. Lee. 1996. "International Measures of Schooling Years and Schooling Quality." *American Economic Review* 86 (2): 218–223.

Barro, R.J. 1999. "Determinants of Economic Growth: Implications of the Global Evidence for Chile." *Cuadernos de Economia* 36 (107): 443–478.

Basu, A., E. Calamitsis, and D. Ghura. 2000. "Promoting Growth in Sub-Saharan Africa: Learning What Works." *IMF Economic Issues* No. 23. http://www.imf.org/external/pubs/ft/issues/issues23/index.htm (August).

Becker, G.S. 1996. *Human Capital*, 3rd edition. Chicago: University of Chicago Press.

Benhabib, J. and M.M. Spiegel. 1994. "The Role of Human Capital in Economic Development: Evidence from Aggregate Cross-Country Data." *Journal of Monetary Economics* 34: 143–173.

Bernard, A.B. and C.I. Jones. 1995. "Technology and Convergence." *The Economic Journal* 106 (437): 1037–1044.

Bertocchi, G. and F. Canova. 1996. "Did Colonization Matter for Growth? An Empirical Exploration into the Historical Causes of Africa's Underdevelopment." http://ideas.repec.org/a/eee/eecrev/v46y2002i10p1851-1871.html.

Bigsten, A. and D. Durevall. 2002. "Is Globalization Good for Africa?" Working Papers in Economics, No. 67. Department of Economics, Gotenborg University (Sweden). http://gupea.ub.gu.se/dspace/bitstream/2077/2841/1/gunwpe0067rev.pdf.

Bloom, D. and J. Sacks. 1998. "Geography, Demography, and Economic Growth in Africa." Harvard Institute for International Development, Harvard University (October Revision).

Boulding, K.E. 1966. "The Economics of Knowledge and the Knowledge of Economics: Richard T. Ely Lecture." *American Economic Review* 56 (1/2): 1–13.

Boyce, J. and L. Ndikumana. 2001. "Is Africa a Net Creditor? New Estimates of Capital Flight from Severely Indebted Sub-Saharan African Countries, 1970–1996." *Journal of Development Studies* 38 (2): 27–56.

Brooks, H. 1994. "The Relationship between Science and Technology." *Research Policy* 23: 477–486.

Bulliet, R.W. 2002. "Religious Conversion and the Spread of Innovations." *Fathom.* http://www.fathom.com/feature/2199/index.html.

Burghes, D.N. and M.S. Borrie. 1981. *Modeling with Differential Equations.* New York: Halsted Press: 63–68.

Campbell, K. 2010. "Africa Rocketing out of Recession." http://www.engineeringnews.co.za/article/africa-rockets-out-of-recession-2010-07-16.

Central Intelligence Agency (CIA) (Various). *Factbooks.* https://www.cia.gov/library/publications/the-worldfactbook/

Charnock, G. and G. Starrosta (eds). 2016. *The New International Division of Labor, Global Transformation and Uneven Development.* New York: International Political Economy Series, Springer Nature, Palgrave Macmillan.

Charrtrand, H.H. 2006. "Ideological Evolution: The Competitiveness of Nations in a Global Knowledge-based Economy. An Individual Interdisciplinary Studies PhD Program." University of Saskatchewan, http://www.culturaleconomics.atfreeweb.com/Dissertation%204/0.0%2)ToC.htm.

Charrtrand, H.H. 2002. "Knowledge-based Economy: Literature Search by Author." http://members.shaw.ca/compilerpress1/KBE%20Lit%20Search%20Author%201.htm.

Cho, Y. and D. Newhouse. 2011. "How Did the GR Affect Different Types of Workers: Evidence from 17 Middle-income Countries." Policy Research Working Paper 5636.

Choi, K. 1983. *Theories of Comparative Economic Growth.* Ames: Iowa State University.

Cipolla, C. 1965. *Guns, Sails and Empires: Technological Innovation and the Early Phases of European Expansion, 1400–1700.* New York: Minerva Press.

Cohn, E. 1979. *The Economics of Education.* Cambridge (MA): Ballinger Publishing Company.

Collier, Paul and Jan Gunning. 1999. "Why Has Africa Grown Slowly?" *Journal of Economic Perspectives* 13 (3): 3–22.

Collier, P. and W. Gunning. 1999. "Explaining African Economic Performance." *Journal of Economic Literature* XXXVII (1): 64–111.

Davis, Graham. 1995 "Learning to Love the Dutch Disease: Evidence from the Mineral Economies. *World Development* 23 (10): 1765–1779.

Deaton, Angus. 1999. "Commodity Prices and Growth in Africa." *Journal of Economic Perspectives* 13 (3): 23–40.

Denison, E. 1967. *Why Growth Rates Differ.* Washington, DC: Brookings Institution.

Desai, M., et. al. 2002. "Measuring Technology Achievement of Nations and the Capacity to Participate in the Network Age." *Journal of Human Development* 3 (1): 95–122.

Desai, M. 2008. "Southern Engines of Global Growth: Very Long Cycles or Short Spurts?" Discussion Paper No. 2008/02. UNU-WIDER (February).
Diamond, J. 1997. *Guns, Germs and Steel: The Fates of Human Societies*. New York: W.W. Norton.
Dixit, A. 2009. "Governance Institutions and Economic Activity." *American Economic Review* 99 (1): 5–24.
Dreher, A., N. Gaston, and P. Martens. 2008. *Measuring Globalization: Gauging Its Consequences*. New York: Springer.
Dreher, A. 2003. "Doe s Globalization Affect Growth?" http://129.3.20.41/eps/dev/papers/0210/0210004.pdf (January Version).
Driouchi, A., E.M. Azelmad, and G.C. Anders. 2006. "An Economic Analysis of the Role of Knowledge in Economic Performance." *Journal of Technology Transfer* 31: 241–255.
Drucker, P.F. 1985. *Innovation and Entrepreneurship: Practice and Principles*. London: Pan Books. Part 1.
Easterly, W. and R. Levine. 1997. "Africa's Growth Tragedy: Politics and Ethnic Divisions." *Quarterly Journal of Economics* CXII (4): 1203–1250.
Easterly, W. and A. Reshef. 2010. "African Export Successes: Surprises, Stylized Facts, and Explanations." NBER Working Paper No. 16597.
Edwards, S., S. Johnson, and D. Weil (eds). 2016. *African Successes*, Volume 1: Governments and Institutions. National Bureau of Economic Research and University of Chicago Press.
Edwards, S., S. Johnson, and D. Weil (eds). 2016. *African Successes*, Volume 2: Human Capital. National Bureau of Economic Research and University of Chicago Press.
Edwards, S., S. Johnson, and D. Weil (eds). 2016. *African Successes*, Volume 3: Modernization and Development. National Bureau of Economic Research and University of Chicago Press.
Edwards, S., S. Johnson, and D. Weil (eds). 2016. *African Successes*, Volume 4: Sustainable Growth. National Bureau of Economic Research and University of Chicago Press.
Fafchamps, M. 2000. "Engines of Growth and Africa's Economic Performance." Department of Economics, University of Oxford. http://www.economics.ox.ac.uk/members/marcel.fafchamps/homepage/engines.pdf (July).
Fagerberg, J. 1995. "Convergence or Divergence: The Impact of Technology on the Growth Rates Differ." *Journal of Evolutionary Economics* 5 (3): 269–284.
Fagerberg, J. 1994. "Technology and International Differences in Growth Rates." *Economic Literature* 32 (3): 1147–1175.
Fagerberg, J., M. Knell, and M. Srholec. 2004. "The Competitiveness of Nations: Economic Growth in the ECE Region." http://www.unece.org/ead/sem/sem2004/papers/Fagerberg.pdf.
Fagerberg, J., M. Srholec, and M. Knell. 2007. "The Competitiveness of Nations: Why Some Countries Prosper While Others Fall Behind." *World Development* 35 (10): 1595–1620.
Fedderke, J. 2001. "Technology, Human Capital and Growth: Evidence from a Middle-income Country Case Study Applying Dynamic Heterogeneous Panel

Analysis." *Annual Forum,* ERSA, University of Witwatersrand, South Africa (September 10–12).

Finfacts.com. 2005. "Global Income Per Capita." http://www.finfacts.com/biz10/globalworldincomepercapita.htm.

Frankel, J. 2010. "Mauritius: African Success Story." NBER Working Paper No. 16569.

Ghura, D. and M.T. Hadjimichael. 1996. "Growth in Sub-Sahara Africa." *IMF Staff Papers* 43 (3): 605–634.

Goklany, I.M. 2002. "The Globalization of Human Well-being." *Policy Analysis*, No. 447. http://www.ato.org/pubs/pas/pa447.pdf (August).

Gordon, R. 2002. "Technology and Economic Performance in the American Economy." www.cepr.org/pubs/dps/DP3213.asp.

Graca, J., S. Jafarey, and A. Philippopoulos. 1995. "Interaction of Hum and Physical Capital in a Model of Endogenous Growth." *Economics of Planning* 28: 93–118.

Gradstein, M. and K.A. Konrad (eds). 2006. "Institutions and Norms in Economic Development." CESifo Seminar Series. Cambridge: MIT Press.

Gupta, B.M., P. Sharma, and C.R. Karisiddappa. 1997. "Growth of Research Literature in Scientific Specialities: A Modeling Perspective." *Scentometrics* 40 (3): 507–528.

Gurak, H. 2004. On Productivity Growth. ICS Stockholm.

Gyimah-Brempong, K. and M. Wilson. 2005. "Human Capital and Economic Growth: Is Africa Different." *Journal of African Development* 7 (1): 73–109.

Gylfason, Thorvaldur and Gylfi Zoega. 2002. "Natural Resource and Economic Growth: The Role of Investment." Central Bank of Chile Working Paper No. 142 (February).

Hall, R. and C.I. Jones. 1999. "Why Do Some Countries Produce So Much More Output per Worker than Others?" *Quarterly Journal of Economics* 114 (1): 83–116.

Harris, D.P. 1992. "Long-term Forecasting for Mineral Industries: Innovative Methods and Case Studies, Lecture Notes." Mineral Economics Program, Department of Mining and Geological Engineering, University of Arizona (January).

Henderson, W.O. 1969. *The Industrialization of Europe, 1780–1914.* New York: Harcourt, Brace, and World Inc. (1970 reprint).

Henderson, J.M. and R.E. Quandt. 1980. *Microeconomic Theory: A Mathematical Approach.* New York: McGraw-Hill International Book Company.

Heston, A., R. Summers, and B. Aten. 2006. "Penn World Table Version 6.2." Center for International Comparisons of Production, Income and Prices at the University of Pennsylvania. http://pwt.econ.upenn.edu/php_site/pwt62/pwt62_form.php (September).

Higgins, M.J., D. Levy, and A.T. Young. 2006. "Growth and Convergence across the Unites States: Evidence from County-level Data." *Reveiw of Economics and Statistics* LXXXVIII (4): 671–681.

Hodder, B.W. 1980. *Economic Development in the Tropics*, 3rd edition. London and New York: Methuen.

Hoselitz, B. 1952. "Non-economic Barriers to Economic Development." *Economic Development and Cultural Change* 1 (1): 8–21.

Hotelling, H. 1925. "A General Mathematical Therory of Depreciation." In *Collected Economics Articles of Harold Hotelling* (1990), edited by Adrian C. Darnell. New York: Springer-Verlag: 36–49.

International Monetary Fund (IMF).Various. *International Financial Statistics Yearbook*. Washington, DC: IMF.

International Monetary Fund (IMF). 2005. *International Financial Statistics Yearbook 2005*. Washington, DC: IMF.

International Monetary Fund (IMF). 2009. *Impact of the Global Financial Crisis on Sub-Saharan Africa*. African Department. IMF.

International Monetary Fund (IMF). 2005. *Economic Outlook: Africa*. http://www.imf.org/eternal/np/sec/pr/2005/pr0586.htm.

Islam, N. 1995. "Growth Empirics: A Panel Data Approach." *Quarterly Journal of Economics* CX (4): 1127–1170.

Islam, N. 2004. "The New Growth Theories: What is in There for Developing Countries?" *Journal of Developing Areas* 38 (1): 170–210.

Jensen, Bill. 2000. *Simplicity: The New Competitive Advantage in a World of More, Better, Faster*. Cambridge (MA): Perseus Books.

Joinafrica.com. Various. "View Africa Rankings." http://www.joinafrica.com/.

Jones, J. 2006. "An Institutional Critique of Recent Attempts to Measure Technological Capability across Countries." *Journal of Economic Issues* XL (3): 743–766.

Jones, B. 2002. "Economic Integration and Convergence of Per Capita Income in West Africa." *African Development Review* 14 (1): 18–47.

Jones, C.I. 1997. "Convergence Revisited." *Journal of Economic Growth* 2 (2): 131–153.

Jones, C.I. 2006. "Knowledge and the Theory of Economic Development." Department of Economics, UC Berkeley. http://www.econ.berkeley.edu~chad.

Jorgenson, D. and K. Vu. 2005. "Information Technology and the World Economy." *Scandinavian Journal of Economics* 107 (4): 631–650.

Jovanovic, B. and Yaw Nyarko. 1995. "The Transfer of Human Capital." *Journal of Economic Dynamics and Control* 19 (September): 1033–1064.

Junod, H.A., 1962. *The Life of a South African Tribe*, Volume II. Mental Life. New Hyde Park (NY): University Books, Inc.

Kaldor, N. 1966. *Causes of the Slow Rate of Growth in the United Kingdom: An Inaugural Lecture*. Cambridge: Cambridge University Press.

Kamarck, Andrew M. 1977. *The Economics of African Development*. New York: Praeger Publishers (Second reprint).

Kamarck, Andrew M. 2000. "Slow Growth in Africa." *Journal Economic Perspectives* 14 (2): 235–236.

Kamarck, Andrew M. 1976. *The Tropics and Economic Development: A Provocative Inquiry*. Baltimore: The John Hopkins University Press.

Kaufmann, D. and A. Kraay. 2008. "Governance Indicators: Where Are We, Where Should We Be Going." *World Bank Observer* 23: 1–30.

Kaufmann, D. and A. Kraay. 2007. "Governance Indicators: Where Are We, Where Should We Be Going." World Bank Policy Research Working Paper 4370.

Kay, J. 2005. *Culture and Prosperity: Why Some Nations Are Rich But Most Remain Poor*. New York: HarperBusiness, Part IV: 266–274.

Keynes, J.M. 1973. *The Collected Works of JM Keynes, Volume III: A Treatise on Probability*. New York: St. Martin's Press.

Kmenta, J. 1986. *Elements of Econometrics*, 2nd edition. New York: Macmillan, Chapter 12: 616–635.

Kneller, R. and P.A. Stevens. 2006. "Frontier Technology and Absorptive Capacity: Evidence from OECD Manufacturing Industries." *Oxford Bulletin of Economics and Statistics* 68 (1): 1–21.

Koch, G.S. and R.F. Lind. 1971. "The Lognormal Distribution." In *Statistical Analysis of Geological Data*. New York: Dover, Chapter 6, Section 6.2: 213–231.

Landes, D. 1998. *The Wealth and Poverty of Nations: Why Some Are So Rich and Some So Poor*. New York: Little Brown.

Lange, G-M. 2004. "Wealth, Natural Capital, and Sustainable Development: Contrasting Examples from Botswana and Namibia." *Environmental and Resource Economics* 29: 257–283.

Lange, M.K. 2004. "British Colonial Legacies and Political Development." *World Development* 32 (6): 905–922.

Laszlo, E. 1972. *The Systems View of the World: The Natural Philosophy of the New Developments in the Sciences*. New York: Georgr Brazilier, Chapter 1.

Leamer, E.E. 2001. "How Much Data, How Much Economics, and How Much Economist in the Stew of Results on the Determinants of Growth?" Lecture at the IMF Institute Economics Training Program Seminar, Washington DC (June 4).

Leamer, E.E. 1983. "Let's Take the Con Out of Econometrics." *American Economic Review* 73: 31–43.

LeBel, P. 1999. "Measuring Sustainable Economic Development in Africa." Department of Economics and Finance, Montclair State University (pdf 2000).

Lee, J-W. 1996. "Government Interventions and Productivity Growth." *Journal of Economic Growth* 1 (3): 391–414.

Lerner, M. 1939. *Ideas Are Weapons: The History and Uses of Ideas*. New York: Viking Press.

Levine, D.L. 1995. *Wealth and Freedom: An Introduction to Political Economy*. New York: Cambridge University Press.

Lewin, K.M. 2000. *Knowledge Matters for Development*. Professorial Lecture. University of Sussex. http://www.sussex.ac.uk/education/documents/knowledge_matters_for_development.pdf

Lewis, W.A. 1954. "Economic Development with Unlimited Supply of Labor." *Manchester School Economic and Social Studies* 20: 139–192.

Lewis, W.A. 1965[1955]. *The Theory of Economic Growth*. New York: Harper Torchbooks.

Los, B. and B. Verspagen. 2001. "The Evolution of Productivity Gaps and Specialization Patterns." http://www.tm.tue.nl/ecis/teg/.

Lucas, R. 1993. "Making a Miracle." *Econometrica* 61 (2): 251–272.

Lucas, R. 1988. "On the Mechanics of Economic Development." *Journal of Monetary Economics* 22 (1): 2–42.

Mankiw, N., D. Romer, and D.N. Weil. 1992. "A Contribution to the Empirics of Economic Growth." *Quarterly Journal of Economics* CVII (2): 407–437.

Marope, M.T. 2005. "Namibia: Human Capital and Knowledge Development for Economic Growth with Equity." Working Paper Series No. 84. Washington, DC: Africa Region Human Development, World Bank.

Marx, K. 1973. *On Society and Social Change*, edited by Neil J. Smelser. Chicago: The University of Chicago press.

Marx, K. 1906. *Capital: A Critique of Political Economy*. New York: The Modern Library.

Masanjala, W.H. and C. Papageorgiu. 2006. "Initial Conditions, European Colonialism and Africa's Growth." Working Paper 2006-01. Department of Economics Working Paper Series. http://www.lsu.edu/economics/papers/pap06_01.pdf.

Masterton-Gibbons, M. 1995. *A Concrete Approach to Mathematical Modelling*. New York: Addison-Wesley.

Maswana, J-C. 2006. "A New Framework for African Economic Development with a Focus on Technological Innovation." Working Paper, WP02/06. Congo Economic Review Notes http://mpra.ub.uni-muenchen.de/5550/1/MPRA_paper_5550.pdf.

Mauro, P. 1998. "Corruption: Causes, Consequences, and Agenda for Further Research." *Finance and Development* (March): 11–14.

Mauro, P. 1995. "Corruption and Growth." *Quarterly Journal of Economics* 110 (3): 681–712.

Max, W. 1947. *The Theory of Social and Economic Organization*, translated by A.M. Henderson and T. Parsons. London: Free Press.

Max, W. 1958. *The Protestant Ethic and the Spirit of Capitalism*. New York: Charles Scribner's Sons.

McCallum, B. 1996. "Neoclassical v. Endogenous Growth Analysis: An Overview." *Federal Reserve Bank of Richmond Economic Quarterly* 82 (4): 41–71.

Meadow, C.T. 1992. *Text Information Retrieval Systems*. San Diego/New York: Academic Press, Inc.

Mishan, E.J. 1974. "Flexibility and Consistency in Project Evaluation." *Economica* 41 (161): 81–96.

Mo Ibrahim Foundation. (Various). "Ibrahim Index of African Governance." http://www.moibrahimfoundation.org/idex/papers.asp.

Mokyr, J. 2005. "Long-term Economic Growth and History of Technology." In: *Handbook of Economic Growth,* Volume 1B, edited by P. Aghion and S.N. Durlauf. New York: Elsevier.

Monga, C. and J. Lin (eds). 2015. *The Oxford Handbook of Africa and Economics: Context and Concepts*, Volume 1. New York and Oxford: Oxford University Press.

Monga, C. and J. Lin (eds). 2015. *The Oxford Handbook of Africa and Economics: Policies and Practices*, Volume 2. New York and Oxford: Oxford University Press.

Mueller, D.C. 1983. *The Political Economy of Growth*. New Haven: Yale University Press.

Nabli, M. 2010. *The Great Recession and Developing Countries: Economic Impact and Growth Prospects*. The World Bank.

Navas-Ruis, A. and Davide Sala. 2007. Technology Adoption and the Selection Effect of Trade." Working Paper, EUIECO, 2007/58. European University Institute.

Ndikumana, L. and J. Boyce. 2011. *Africa's Odious Debts: How Foreign Loans and Capital Flight Bled a Continent*. London: Zed Books.

Ndulu, B. and S. O'Connell. 1999. "Governance and Growth in Sub-Saharan Africa." *Journal of Economic Perspectives* 13 (3): 41–66.

Nelson, R.R. 2002. "Technology, Institutions, and Innovation Systems." *Policy Research* 31 (2): 262–272.

Nepembe, M., M. Mabvuto, and A. Chaka. 2007. "Comparing Retail Banking Changes in Namibia, South Africa and Botswana." Windhoek: Nepru Policy Brief, Issue 19.

Nicolson, S. and I. Tjizake. n.d. "Namibian Research Capacity: An Analysis and Recommendations." Directorate of Research, Science and Technology, Ministry of Higher Education, Training and Employment Creation, Windhoek.

North, D. 1990. *Institutions, Institutional Change, and Economic Performance*. Cambridge: Cambridge University Press.

North, D.C. 1966. *The Economic Growth of the United States, 1790–1860*. New York: W.W. Norton and Company.

Nunn, N. 2005. "Historical Lagacies: A Model Linking Africa's Past to Its Current Underdevelopment." Working Paper, Department of Economics, University of British Columbia. http://ideas.repec.org/p/wpa/wuwpdc/0508008.html.

Nunn, N. 2004. "Slavery, Institutional Development, and Long-run Growth in Africa, 1400–2000." http://ideas.repec.org/p/wpa/wuwpit/0411007.html.

Nunn, N. and d. Puga. 2012, "Ruggedness: The Blessing of Bad Geography in Africa." *Review of Economics and Statistics* 94 (1): 20–36.

O'Connell, S. and B. Ndulu. 2000. "Africa's Growth Experience: A Focus on Sources of Growth." http://www.gdnet.org/pdf/422_O_Connell-Ndulu2.pdf (April).

OECD. 2005. "Africa's Economy: Aid and Growth." *OECD Observer*. http://www.oecdobserver.org/news (July).

OECD. 2005. *African Economic Outlook*. Paris: Development Centre. www.oecd-bookshop.org.

Parente, S.L. and E. Prescott. 1994. "Barriers to Technology Adoption and Development." *Journal of Political Economy* 102 (2): 298–321.

Persson, T. and G. Tabellini. 2003. *Economic Effects of Constitutions*. Cambridge (MA): MIT Press.

Persson, T. 2005. "Forms of Democracy, Policy and Economic Development." Institute for International Economic Studies, Stockholm University. http://www.iies.su.se/~persson/.

Pitchford, J. 2002. "Trevor Swan's 1956 Economic Growth Seminar and Notes on Economic Growth." *Economic Record* 78: 381–387.

Polanyi, K. 1957. *The Great Transformation*. Boston: Beacon Press.

Quibria, M. 2006. "Does Governance Matter? Yes, No or Maybe: Some Evidence from Developing Asia." *Kyklos* 59 (1): 99–114.

Robinson, J.A. 2009. "Botswana As a Role Model for Country Success." UNU-WIDER Research Paper 2009/40 (June).

Rodriguez, F. and Jeffrey Sachs. 1999. "Why Do Resource-abundant Economies Grow More Slowly?" *Journal of Economic Growth* 4: 277–303.

Rodrik, D., A. Subramanian, and F. Trebbi. 2004. "Institutions Rule: The Primacy of Institutions over Geography and Integration in Economic Development." *Journal of Economic Growth* 9 (2): 131–165.

Rodrik, D. 1997. *Has Globalization Gone Too Far?* Washington, DC: Institute for International Economics.

Rodrik, D. 2012. *Globalization Paradox.: Democracy and the Future of the World Economy*. New York: W.W. Norton.

Rogers, E. 1983. *Diffusion of Innovations*, 3rd edition. London: Free Press.

Rogers, E. 2003. *Diffusion of Innovations*, 5th edition. London: Free Press.

Rogers, M. 2003. "A Survey of Economic Growth." *Economic Record* 79 (244): 112–135.

Romer, P.M. 2010. "Technologies, Rules, and Progress: The Case for Charter Cities." Center for Global Development. www.cgdev.org/content/publications/detail/1423916.

Romer, P.M. 1993. "Idea Gaps and Object Gaps in Economic Development." *Journal of Monetary Economics* 32 (3): 543–573.

Romer, P. 1990. "Endogenous Technological Change." *Journal of Political Economy* 98 (5): S71–S102.

Romer, P.M. n.d. "Economic Growth." In *The Fortune Encyclopedia of Economics*, edited by David R. Henderson: Warner Book. http://dipeco.economia.unimib.it/persone/colombo/silsis/Economic%20Growth%20encyclopedia.htm.

Romer, P.M. 1994. "The Origins of Endogenous Growth Theory." *Journal of Economic Perspectives* 8 (1): 3–22.

Rosenberg, N. 1982. *Inside the Black-box: Technology and Economics*. New York: Cambridge University Press.

Russell, B. 1948. *Human Knowledge: Its Scope and Limit*. New York: Simon and Schuster.

Russell, B. 1956. *Logic and Knowledge: Essays 1901–1950*, edited by Robert C. Marsh. New York: Capricorn Books.

Sachs, J. and A.M. Warner. 1997. "Sources of Slow Growth in African Economies." *Journal of African Economies* 6 (3): 335–376.

Sachs, Jeffrey and Andrew Warner. 1999. "The Big Push, Natural Resource Booms and Growth." *Journal of Development Economics* 59: 43–76.

Sampat, B.N. 2006. "The Dismal Science and the Endless Frontier." http://www.tpac.gatech.edu/nsfworkshop/essays/Sampat.pdf.

Sampat, B.N. 2005. "The Dismal Science and the Endless Frontier: How and Why Economists Think about S & T Policy: A Guide for Further Reading." http://ideas.repec.org/p/wpa/wuwpit/0411007.html.

Samuelson, P.A. 1994. "The Classical Fallacy." *Journal of Economic Literature* XXXII (June): 620–639.

Samuelson, L. 2004. "Modeling Knowledge in Economic Analysis." *Journal of Economic Literature* XLII (2): 367–403.

Sarokin, D. and J. Schulkin. 2016. *Missed Information: Better Information for Building a Wealthier, more Sustainable Future*. Cambridge and London: MIT Press.
Schultz, T. Paul. 1999. "Heath and Schooling Investments in Africa." *Journal of Economic Perspectives* 13 (3): 67–88.
Schultz, T.W. 1981. *Investing in People: The Economics of Population Quality*. Berkeley: University of California Press.
Schumpeter, J.A. 1954. *History of Economic Analysis*. New York: Oxford University Press.
Schumpeter, J.A. 2005. "Development." *Journal of Economic Literature* 43 (1): 108–120.
Segal, A. 1985. "Africa: Frustration and Failure." In *Learning by Doing: Science and Technology in the Developing World*. Westview Special Studies in Science, Technology, and Public Policy, Chapter 5, 107–127.
Sender, John. 1999. "Africa's Economic Performance: Limitations of the Current Consensus." *Journal of Economic Perspectives* 13 (3): 89–114.
Sheppard, E. 2016. *Limits to Globalization: Disruptive Geographies of Capitalist Development*. Oxford and New York: Oxford University Press.
Siba, E.G. 2008. "Determinants of Institutional Quality in Sub-Saharan African Countries." Working Papers in Economics, University of Gothenburg. http://gupea.ub.gu.se/dspace/bitstream/2077/10382/1/gunwpe0310.pdf.
Smith, A. 1976[1776]. *An Inquiry into the Nature and Causes of the Wealth of Nations*, edited by Edwin Cannan. Chicago: University of Chicago Press.
Soderbom, M. and F. Teal. 2003. "Openness and Human Capital as Sources of Productivity Growth: An Empirical Investigation." CSAE/WPS/2003-06, Department of Economics, University of Oxford. (May).
Solow, R.M. 1957. "Technical Change and the Aggregate Production Function." *Review of Economics and Statistics* 39: 312–320.
Solow, R.M. 1956. "A Contribution to the Theory of Economic Growth." *Quarterly Journal of Economics* LXX: 65–94.
Solow, R.M. 1997. *Learning from 'Learning by doing': Lessons for Economic Growth*. The Kenneth J. Arrow Lectures. Stanford: Stanford University Press.
Sowell, T. 1996. *Knowledge and Decisions*. New York: Basic Books.
Springer, C.L., R.R. Herlihy, R.T. Mall, and R.I. Beggs. 1968. *Probabilistic Models,* Volume 4 of Mathematics for Management Series. Homewood (IL): Richard D. Irwin, Inc, Chapter 8.
Ssozi, J., S. Asongu, and V. Amavilah. 2019. "The Effectiveness of Development Aid for Agriculture in Sub-Saharan Africa." *Journal of Economic Studies* 46(20): 284–305.
Stamp, L.D. 1953. *Africa: A Study in Tropical Development*. New York: John Wiley & Sons, Inc.
Stigler, G.J. 1984. *The Intellectual and the Marketplace*. Enlarged edition. Cambridge (MA): Harvard University Press.
Stiglitz, J.E. 1986. "Economics of Information and the Theory of Economic Development." NBER Working Paper Series, Vol. W1566. http://ssrn.com/abstract=336315.

Stiglitz, J.E. 2000. "The Contributions of the Economics of Information to Twentieth Century Economics." *Quarterly Journal of Economics* 115 (4): 1441–1477.

Subramanian, A. 2009. "The Mauritian Success Story and Its Lessons." UN-WIDER Research Paper 2009/36. (June).

Swan, T. 2002. "Economic Growth." *Economic Record* 78: 375–380.

Swan, T. 1956. "Economic Growth and Capital Accumulation." *Economic Record* 32: 334–361.

Tahari, A., D. Ghura, B. Akitoby, and E. Aka. 2004. "Sources of growth in Sub-Saharan Africa." IMF Working Paper, WP/04/176. http://internationalmonetaryfund.com/external/pubs/ft/wp/2004/wp04176.pdf (September).

Takeda, H. (ed). *Micro-performance During Postwar Japan's High Growth Era: Monography Series of the Socio-Economic History Society of Japan.* New York: Springer Nature.

Taylor, L.D. 2000. *Capital, Accumulation, and Money: An Integration of Capital, Growth, and Monetary Policy.* New York: Kluwer Academic Publishers.

Taylor, J.E. and R.E. Levitt. 2004. "A New Model for Systemic Innovation Diffusion in Project-based Industries." CIFE Working Paper #WP086. Stanford University. http://www.stanford.edu/group/CIFE/online.publications/WP086.pdf.

Teller, Ed. 1981. *The Pursuit of Simplicity.* Malibu (CA): Pepperdine University Press.

Temple, J. 1999. "The New Growth Evidence." *Journal of Economic Literature* XXXVII (1): 112–156.

Temple, J. and P. Johnson. 1998. "Social Capability and Economic Growth." *Quarterly Journal of Economics* CXIII (3): 965–990.

Thirlwall, A.P. 1978. *Growth and Development*, 2nd edition. London: Macmillan Press Ltd.

Thompson, L. 1969. *African Societies in Southern Africa.* New York: Praeger Publishers: 3.

Thompson, D.W. 1942[1992]. *On Growth and Form*, The complete revised edition. New York: Dover Publications, Inc.

Toynbee, A. 1959. *A Study of History.* New York: Oxford University Press, Chapters 11 and 12.

United Nations Economic Commission for Africa (UNECA). 2006. *Annual Report 2006.* http://www.uneca.org/conferenceofministers/2006/documents.htm (April).

United Nations Economic Commission for Africa (UNECA).Various. *Annual Reports.* http://www.uneca.org/conferenceofministers/.

United Nations Economic Commission for Africa (UNECA). 2008. "Survey of Economic and Social Conditions in Africa in 2007." http://www.uneca.org/cfm/2008/docs/survery-ecosocial07.pdf

U.N. Development Programme (UNDP). 2003–2011. *Human Development Reports.* http://hdr.undp.org/reports/global/.

Urban, G.L. and J.R. Hauser. 1980. *Design and Marketing of New Products.* Englewood Cliffs (NJ): Prentic-Hall, Inc, Chapters 5, 11, 14, 15, and 16.

Velde, D.W. 2009. "The Global Financial Crisis: Impact, Responses, and Way Forward." United Nations Economic Commission for Africa (UNECA).

Verick, S. and I. Islam. 2010. "The GR of 2008–2009: Causes, Consequences and Policies Responses." IZA, DP No. 4934 (May).

von Bertalanffy, L. 1968. *General System Theory: Foundations, Development, Applications*, Revised edition. New York: George Braziller.

von Hayek, F.A. 1937. "Economics and Knowledge." *Economica* (New Series) 4 (13): 33–54.

von Hayek, F.A. 1974. "The Pretense of Knowledge—Nobel Memorial Lecture." *American Economic Review* 79 (6): 3–7.

Warsh, D. 2006. *Knowledge and the Wealth of Nations: A Story of Economic Discovery*. New York: W.W. Norton and Company.

Waters, M. 1995. *Globalization*. New York: Routledge.

Wejnert, B. 2002. "Integrating Models of Diffusion of Innovations: A Conceptual Framework." *Annual Reviews of Sociology* 28: 297–326.

Whitehead, A.N. 1929. *The Aims of Education and Other Essays*. New York: Free Press.

Wickelgren, W.A. 1995. *How to Solve Mathematical Problems*. New York: Dover Publications, Inc.

World Bank. Various. *World Governance Indicators*. 1996–2007. http://info.worldbank.org/governance/wgi2007/ and www.worldbank.org/wbi/governance/.

World Bank. Various. *World Development Indicators*. Washington, DC: World Bank.

World Bank. n.d. *Economic Development and the Quality of Legal Institutions*. http://www1.worldbank.org/publicsector/legal/institutional.htm

World Bank. 2001. *A Chance to Learn: Knowledge and Finance for Education in Su- Saharan Africa*. African Region Human Development Series. http://www-wds.worldbank.org/servlet/WDSContentServer/WDSP/IB/2001/04/24/00009494601032905304794/Rendered/PDF/multi0page.pdf.

World Bank. 1993. *The East Asian Miracle: Economic Growth and Public Policy – Summary*. World Bank Policy Research Report. Washington, DC: World Bank.

World Bank. Various. *Country classification, Data and Statistics*. http?//web.worldbank.org/WEBSITE/EXTERNAL/DATASTATISTICS/

World Bank. 1989. *Sub-Saharan Africa: From Crisis to Sustainable Growth: A Long-Term Perspective Study*. Washington, DC: World Bank.

World Economic Forum. Various. *Global Competitiveness Reports*. https://www.weforum.org/reports.

World Resource Institute. 2005. "National Savings: Gross National Savings, Percent of GNI." http://earthtrends.wri.org/searchable_db/results.php?years=.

Worldfactsandfigures.com. 2005. "GDP Per Capita by Country." http://www.worldfactsandfigures.com/gdp_country_desc.php.

Young, H.P. 2005. "The Spread of Innovations by Social Learning." Working Paper. http://www.econ.jhu.edu/People/Young/Spread28march.pdf (February 17, 2006 Version).

Young, H.P. 2004. "Innovation Diffusion and Population Heterogeneity." Preliminary Draft, Johns Hopkins University. http://www.econ.princeton.edu/seminars/SEMINARS/Fall06Seminars/young.pdf (October 20, 2006 Version)

Young, H.P. 2007. “Innovation Diffusions in Heterogeneous Populations.” Discussion Paper Series, No. 303. Department of Economics, University of Oxford. http://www.economics.ox.ac.uk/Research/wp/pdf/paper303.pdf.

Young, A. 1928. “Increasing Returns and Economic Progress.” *Economic Journal* 38: 527–542.

Young, A. 2012. “The African Growth Miracle.” *Journal of Political Economy* 120 (4): 696–739.

Index

Note: Page numbers in italics denotes figures and tables; page numbers followed by "n" denote end notes.

About the Author

Voxi Heinrich Amavilah has published in internationally recognized journals on the economic performance of African and other developing economies. His current research focuses on the implications of the knowledge economy on the economic performance of developing and emerging economies, utilizing modern economic and econometric analysis, as well as clustering and machine deep learning neural network techniques. An adjunct professor of economics at Estrella Mountain College, Dr. Amavilah received his BA in economics from UCLA, his MS in agricultural and resource economics from Oregon State University, and his PhD in mineral economics from the University of Arizona.

www.ingramcontent.com/pod-product-compliance
Ingram Content Group UK Ltd.
Pitfield, Milton Keynes, MK11 3LW, UK
UKHW020842290926
15470UKWH00004B/1499

9 781498 597838